C000243323

Dryi__g Herbs

The Only Herb Drying Book You'll Ever Need

(A Quick Guide on Easily Drying Herbs for Everyday Kitchen Spices)

Danny Horvath

Published By **Tyson Maxwell**

Danny Horvath

All Rights Reserved

Drying Herbs: The Only Herb Drying Book You'll Ever Need (A Quick Guide on Easily Drying Herbs for Everyday Kitchen Spices)

ISBN   978-1-77485-700-7

Legal & Disclaimer

TABLE OF CONTENTS

Introduction

It's no secret that plants have been utilized for their health benefits and nutrition for millennia. The fact that they're still employed in many civilizations around the globe is proof of their benefits to health. When you shop at the supermarket you could be charged a lot for fresh herbs that are not of the highest quality.

It's impossible to be sure the quality of what you're buying. There are websites that claim they are the top quality. But who says that? How can you tell the truth? Some websites are legitimate and others are trying to make a big profit through your inexperience. Finding the most affordable price and of top quality can be difficult, but not impossible.

Another option to buy herbs is to grow your own and then harvesting the herbs. They're fun to cultivate and aren't expensive. They're not even requiring much maintenance, and they'll be ready to be used at any time you're at your best. In this guide, you'll learn about the process of harvesting, drying and storing your herbs in order that they can be later prepared and served.

For growing herbs, you won't require any space, since it's not necessary to have a large garden. It is possible to plant your herbs outside, however, they could also fit on the windowsill of your kitchen. There is no need to devote lots of time maintaining them.

However, you will require the time and energy in getting your plants started right. They require the proper amount of sunlight and water. It is also necessary to periodically trim them to ensure that dead foliage doesn't take essential nutrients from the healthy plant.

The process of drying is important to be aware of. If herbs aren't dried correctly they could turn to become moldy and ruined. Incorrectly dried herbs won't provide the same quality you'd like or anticipate.

You may be accepting the importance of herbs, yet insisting that you can't cultivate the plants yourself. Many times, people avoid anything that is new. Instead, be brave and take advantage of this chance. Beginning is the first step to reap the full advantages. It's your choice.

Additionally, it's not that easy to make dried herbs and this book can guide you through a myriad of possibilities. The method you decide to use is often a matter of to your own personal preference. It is also possible to test a few different options and determine which one is most compatible for your specific needs.

It isn't necessary to have a degree in order to cultivate the herbs and then dry them. But, it is important to know the basics of the processes involved. Proper storage is equally crucial as drying the herbs. The most important thing is having the herbs available for use anytime you need them.

You'll be delighted with the outcomes of cultivating and drying the herbs you have grown yourself. You'll be aware of the exact ingredients that make up your food, their nutritional value, and their medicinal uses. In a world where many of the items you buy from stores are treated with pesticides and chemicals homemade foods could offer you peace of mind.

Chapter 1: What Is Drying? Herbs Is

Important

Drying herbs correctly is crucial so that they don't lose their medicinal or nutritional value. It's not sensible to spend the time to plant and harvest them, and then abandon the ball when drying and storage.

Prevention

In order to prevent yeast, mold and bacteria from forming on your herbs is crucial. This can be achieved by eliminating all water from them. The problem is that moisture cannot be visible but its presence will be soon apparent as soon as you open a jar , or bag of dried herbs, they'll be destroyed. The smell and color will immediately tell you if something isn't the way it should be. When they are dried completely however, you won't experience this problem.

Accessibility

It is almost impossible to have fresh herbs available. They're not able to last for long. When you dry them in the sun, they'll be available to be used whenever you want. They're accessible from the comfort of your home rather than going to the market to buy fresh herbs.

You'll also feel comfortable knowing that the herbs were grown without the use of chemicals. It's not possible to be certain when purchasing dried plants from a retailer. If you're looking for something 100% natural, you need to be certain of the source of it.

Ideally, you will want to plant enough herbs to get through the winter and autumn months. If you do this you will keep enough herbs until springtime in which you can begin again with the cultivation and harvesting of new herbs. Do not store dried herbs for longer than a year because they'll begin losing their worth. It is difficult initially to determine the amount you'll consume over the course of a calendar year, but try your best to assess.

Take note of the frequency and amount you're using your herbs right now and in the beginning of your year, to make adjustments for the next year. If you require more, you should keep different plants in different stages of development. You don't have to start over again and wait until you've got additional herbage available.

Cost

You'll spend considerably lesser drying the herbs you grow than purchasing them. In actual fact, you'll pay less for the whole process of cultivating them, harvesting them drying them and then storing them than purchasing them.

If you regularly use herbs it will help you save money and make much sense. If you know more about the health benefits various herbs can provide, you'll likely to consider using them more often than you currently do. A savings in money is an advantage that you shouldn't ignore.

Furthermore, what happens do you do if you suffer from a chronic health issue because of diet-related deficiencies? Then you'll have to spend more money on medical visits, copays, prescriptions and deductibles. Certain herbs can help to prevent diseases, which could result in more money that stays in your pocket.

Health Benefits

Different varieties of herbs can provide either medicinal or nutritional value. Some have both! It is crucial to know these characteristics when you are thinking about the process of growing and harvesting, drying and even storing them.

Spend time studying cases and other information from reliable books or websites. You'll find that, over and over again results show that taking various herbs improves the quality of life and helps to reduce the signs of any health issue.

The modern world of medicine might not be able to fully comprehend the value of herbs, but they should not overlook the value that they provide. It's also true that over the centuries, our ancestors used herbs and natural remedies to survive.

When you utilize herbs in the manner prescribed, there is no risk to your health. When you are making oils from plants keep in mind that they're very powerful. A couple of drops will be enough! With all this in mind, you've got absolutely nothing to gain by giving these herbs to try.

Nutritional Value

Many cook with herbs due to the fact that they love their flavours. However, these flavors originated because the herbs provided the nutritional value.

Our ancestors weren't eating processed food or large quantities of sugar. They worked hard every day to ensure their survival. The food they consumed was selected to provide them with the highest nutritional value. It was not just to meet their body's requirements, but also to lower the chance of developing health issues also.

Cinnamon, for instance helps to boost the metabolism. This in turn helps regulate blood sugar levels. This is particularly the case in those who experience an increase in blood sugar levels following meals.

Dried cloves, on other hand, provide potent antioxidants. They reduce the chance of health problems and may help your body to perform at its best.

Here are few examples that herbs could assist you feel more relaxed and also enhance the taste of your meals. Everyone needs to eat and drink, so why not choose food that is healthy and delicious?

The Medicinal Value

The dried ginger powder is anti-inflammatory and is an excellent example of a plant with immense medicinal worth. It may help in reducing the discomfort and pain that are often caused by various types of arthritis.

With all the fantastic information available increasing numbers of people are choosing to make use of dried herbs for therapeutic value. This could help them save money on expensive drugs. They can also to avoid the severe adverse effects of these medications.

But this isn't to say that using dried herbal remedies is an effective replacement for medical treatment. Be careful not to diagnose or treat yourself or other people. Always work with medical professional to determine and treat health problems.

Do not be afraid to tell your doctor you are using herbs for medicinal reasons too.

Although they may not prescribe specific herbs but they shouldn't advise you not to take herbs. It's important to communicate with your physician in a transparent manner to let them know the kind of medicine you're taking as well as how frequently.

Remember that many societies survived for hundreds of years making use of plants. They didn't have hospitals or other institutions where patients could seek treatment as we do. Many people are drawn to the concept to "going back to basic" and staying away from pharmaceuticals.

There are a few general rules to be followed in the event that you want to grow and harvest medicinal herbs. These are:

* Making the right herbal choices for your health requirements.

* Make sure that the soil you plant them doesn't contain a lot of toxic chemicals.

Pick your herbs in the middle of the morning or before noon so that the condensation has dissolved. (Dew can increase the chance for mold.)

Chapter 2: Choosing Herbs To Dry

After you've decided on the plants to plant You must follow the guidelines for them meticulously. Some require more sun or water than others. Take note of how they appear and make changes to your routine of care in the event that things aren't going as planned.

Label your herbs before you start planting them. This is since many of them look similar when they begin to develop. It is important to be certain that you know what a particular herb is before using it for your nutritional value or therapeutic purposes.

It's also crucial to keep an eye on the leaves of the plants as they develop. It is important to regularly get rid of any part of the plant which appear to be damaged or ill. If you notice that the stem has discolored, the leaves are deflating or the plant is covered with black spots, it's obvious that there's a problem that shouldn't be overlooked.

Certain herbs have to be pulled, while some require cutting. There are others which require plucked. Making sure you use the correct technique is crucial to not harm or damage the harvest. It is essential to have sharp knives and sharp cutting blades for the job.

Utilize the Whole Plant

Do not throw away the plant, and only use its roots. Certain kinds of herbs work that way. You must ensure that you are aware of the correct information about the herb you're working with. The method you use to harvest one herb might not be appropriate one for another.

Pick the leaves that look the most healthy for harvest. The older leaves won't be able give you the same worth. They can be collected and use them to make mulch to your lawn so they don't end up in the trash. Based on the kind of herbs you're cultivating, you could be making use of:

* Leaves
* stems
* seeds

* flower-heads
* Bark
* Roots

When is the best time to harvest?

Deciding when to cut and pick the herb can be a challenge initially. If you cut them too early, the yield could be insufficient and if you're late, your plants might be damaged. Planting them in tiny pots can be the most efficient way to keep an check on the plants.

Every herb is different in the time it is ready for harvest. This means that you should be aware of the specifics of the specific herbs you're cultivating. As you begin your journey you should limit yourself to not more than three different herbs. This will allow you to concentrate on them and not feel overwhelmed.

As your comfort level and knowledge increases as you get more comfortable, you can grow more plants . It is important to learn the basics down, and also manage your time. Otherwise, all your efforts invest in developing them will end up being a loss.

Many of the herbs people cultivate are plants that produce seeds. After the seeds are developed they will cease to develop. They've fulfilled their goal. Pick the leaves regularly to stimulate more foliage to develop before the seeds begin to sprout. The most common herbs are the chives, basil, and parsley.

Basil requires cutting regularly during the process of growing. If you let it develop untamed, it can be stretched out. If you cut it back, you'll observe that the plant is growing both upwards and outwards. It will also change to a deep green shade. It is harvested when it's about twelve" tall and has a lot of green leaves.

Chives can grow quickly. They are most prolific in spring and the summer. If you are a frequent user you can plant them in different pots in various dates. This will allow you to dry and harvest some while others are growing and will be ready for harvest within a few weeks.

Parsley can be a challenge to cut off when getting ready for pick. Take the entire leaf and place it on the stalk. Cut it around the point that it starts to clump. Leaves that are older tend to become hard and should not be cut.

It is essential to pick rosemary before it turns hard and woody. The shoots should be cut back, but do not cut through the branches that are woody or lacking leaves. It is possible to dry rosemary in a jumble So don't fret even if you gather a amount in one go.

The most effective method to harvest basil is using scissors that are securely held between your thumb and fingers. Cut just above the leaves to see the new growth. If you cut just below one of the leaves and the stem is too short to continue growing. In the end, however, it'll wilt away and you'll need take it back.

Capsicum must be cut off when it turns color. Most people cut it off when it's still green. If you're cautious, your plant may begin to change color, turning red and orange. The time is when you can pick it. You should be extremely cautious when handling the stems since they can be quite tough.

Mint is among the easiest plants to grow and pick. Take a snip of healthy, mature leaves.

This allows it to to grow and allow you to collect more as you require it.

Oregano is a herb with very small roots, so it is important to be cautious when using these roots. It is among the herbs in which you are advised to cut off the older leaves and apply the snipped leaves. Leave the younger leaves to remain in place so that they will keep growing and flourish.

By slicing the sage, cut off the leaves that are still soft. But, you shouldn't try to cut off more than half from the plant. In the event that you cut it too much, it will not create new leaves in the future. It is best to harvest it early in the day , when it is dry due to the dew. But don't keep waiting until it gets too hot, or the vital oils will get dried out due to the heat of the sun.

Thyme is another plant that has very small roots, therefore you must pick it carefully. Make use of a pair of scissors to remove the items you require. Make sure not to use excessive force, otherwise you could damage your entire tree.

When you harvest shallots cut them from the outside and work your way inside. The middle of the plant is filled with new shoots sprouting. They will replace the outer leaves that you cut off.

It's not an exhaustive checklist, therefore don't be concerned when you don't find the guidelines for the plants you're planning to grow. Doing a little online research will provide you with the most effective methods for growing and harvesting different plants. You can also view step-by-step videos on the internet, which can be extremely helpful in the beginning stages of learning how to cultivate your own herb garden.

Chapter 3: Preparing For The Drying Process

The things you have to prepare for drying will depend on the method you choose to use. Do not worry about it, there is no need to purchase costly equipment, or something similar to that. A majority of people have all they require already at their homes.

Time

The length of time is crucial for drying herbs since it is impossible to speed up the process. It is crucial to dry your herbs the proper method. If you don't want to wait for this process, it's not worth beginning. Be aware that this process could take longer in the initial instances you collect. Once you've done that, you'll be able to complete the task more quickly and effectively.

Supplies

The equipment you require will depend on the method you intend to employ for drying. The details of the options in a subsequent chapter, and you can then decide.

If you intend to hang your herbs to dry, you'll require twine.

Also, you will require burlap bags or cheese cloth. These are used to cover the herbs to ensure that they don't deprive them of their potency. The UV rays keep them to dry out, but too much exposure can reduce the potency of the herb.

If you intend to bake in the oven it will require multiple baking sheets. This will allow you to place herbs in one layer. You can make use of dehydrators with tray options or a microwave.

Some people prefer using gloves to avoid touching the herb directly. Buy disposable gloves so that you can put them off and on during the process whenever you want to. It is possible to purchase a pack of gloves that are disposable for couple of dollars.

Packaging and Labeling

Also, you will require containers or bags for storing dried herbs efficiently. The bags should be clearly labeled. This will be discussed in greater detail in a later chapter.

It is not necessary to have large jars unless your plan is to utilize your herbs in massive quantities. There are small glass jars with cork lids. They look beautiful and do not take up much space. They are easy to label and have them readily easy to access.

Work Space

It is essential to have ample space for work to harvest your plants. An island counter in the kitchen or table are great options. Be sure to wipe everything down and dried prior to when you begin making use of the herbs.

If you're making use of a method to dry that takes several weeks, you'll need remain in the space for the appropriate amount of time. It's this problem with space that leads people to choose quicker methods for drying their herbs that include the dehydrator or oven.

But, if they are hung to dry the clothes won't consume much room. You'll need to use your workspace again, however once they're dry. That's when you're going to break them up and pack them.

Cleaning and washing

You must wash the herbs you've collected before drying them. Make use of a brush that has stiff bristles that gently clean away the soil and any remaining residue. Nail brushes are the best since it's tiny and is able to fit comfortably around your fingers to give you a great grip.

Cleanse the dirt and residue with warm water. Make sure to dry the herbs with paper towels to eliminate any excess water. You may also let drying the herb on towels placed on the counter while working with other people.

A few people do not bother with this part of the washing procedure. They think it will cause the herbs dry more quickly. But, if you don't clean them, there is a risk of residue and dirt entering your food items while cooking using them.

The washing process shouldn't take longer than a few minutes and you can lightly pat the herbs dry using paper towels. Do not skimp this step to try to shorten the time required drying your herb. It will be a regret later that you'd spent the time to finish it!

Extractions

In the case of the use of herbal remedies it is possible to extract the fluids out of the plants. In this way, you will not actually use the plant material, like leaves or stems. There are three methods to extract you can apply. The method you select can be a choice depending on your needs, preference and/or the kind of plant you're extracting from. It's a good idea to look at the three options before making a decision. There are three choices:

* Infusion
* Decoction
* Tincture

Infusion

There is a possibility of hearing the term infusion and tisane interchangeably. It is among the most commonly used and fastest extraction methods. It requires:

* a small iron skillet
* A glass pitcher
* A tea strainer
* A household scale

Do not use pans constructed from copper or aluminum. They could release particles into the digestive tract. They also can cause herbs to develop a bitter taste.

Add around a pint of cool water in the pot. Then heat until the water is boiling and then shut off the heating. Add the herb into the water while it's still hot, but not boiling. The herbs should be stirred gently until they are completely submerged, but take careful not to scratch them.

Allow the plants to stay inside the water for around 10 minutes. Transfer the mixture through the strainer and into the pitcher made of glass. If you are using certain plants, you might have to strain them three or four times due to their strength. Be sure to read the information below for the herb you're working with.

Decoction

Another popular method of making medicinal herbs is through decoction. This isn't difficult to master however many people discover that to master it, they must practice frequently. This is a great technique to employ when you're looking to create tiny amounts of medication.

Put an one ounce of dried herb in an oven with 1 pint of water. bring to a boil. Reduce the temperature and let the liquid continue to cook. Monitor it, and remove it from the flame when the volume of liquid in the pan has been reduced to approximately 1/4 of the liquid originally.

Strain it thoroughly. In general, this method is employed when extracting bark or the roots of plants. If you require a substantial quantity of the element that you extract it is not the ideal option to go with.

Tincture

This method of extracting from plants, you'll employ alcohol rather than water since it's more effective. It helps draw out more of the medicinal benefits than water does. This is the reason why herbalists soak the plants in alcohol prior to make use of the plants.

Do not use methanol or wood alcohol to perform this extraction method. This could result in someone becoming very sick, or be killed. Take about one teaspoon of the plant in one pint alcohol for eight weeks. Shake the container every daily for four weeks. Let it remain for the following four weeks. Strain thoroughly towards the close of the 8 week time period.

Chapter 4: Drying Methods

There are many options for drying the herbs. Certain people use a particular method that they employ every day. Others, it is contingent on the kind of herb they are using. You should also consider a couple of options before deciding which one is best for you.

Whatever method or technique you decide to employ, don't be afraid! Drying herbs is a lot easier than you'd imagined. Spend some time learning the basics, and you'll be able to do it. When are they dry?

It is essential to give the herb enough time to completely dry. They are completely dry when they're brittle and fall apart easily. Do not crush them until you're actually in a position to utilize the leaves.

Remember that if your herbs aren't dry enough they could be prone to mold , and various issues. In the end, you'll have to throw them away instead of benefiting from the efforts. Allow them to have the space they require to fully dry, and you'll be pleased with the result.

Basic Tips

Before we get into the drying process itself here are some general guidelines I'd like to provide to you. They will help you understand the reason why you dry in specific ways.

Drying is a method used by the early civilizations to preserve herbs. While the technique may be ancient, that does not mean it's ineffective. According to the old saying, you don't need to reinvent the wheel to achieve results that are effective!

As was mentioned in a prior chapter, make sure you ensure that you clean your herbs prior to starting drying them. Don't let dust and residue to sit.

Do not use pesticides for your plants as well. This can lead to the presence of toxins , even after washing them. Utilize all-natural methods to grow your plants for the greatest overall results. It is important to dry them properly after rinsing. It is essential for all water on the surface to be removed.

Examine the plants that you are preparing to dry. If you notice any indications of decay or dead leaves it is time to take it off. If it is left untreated, it could cause damage to the plants.

In the Sunlight

It is possible to arrange your herbs in small bundles, and then tie them by string. Place them upside down on your porch, in a location in which they can get plenty of sun. Make sure that your bundles aren't too tight, or air won't be able circulate around them.

Since UV rays may discolor the plants and can decrease their effectiveness, you should consider protecting them with a cloth. This can be done with an old burlap bag that's broken into smaller pieces. It is tied around the plants when they're drying, and allow air and sunlight to touch but not harm the plants. You can hang them out to dry inside your house in a space which is air-conditioned. The space should also be well lit. The attic is an excellent option due to its proximity than the sunlight. The basement however will not work because of the lack of sunlight. In addition, basements can be damp and humidity won't allow your plants to dry properly.

It may take a few weeks to dry herbs in this manner. Within a few weeks, you should check the herbs every day. If they do not crumble when you press them, give them another day and then check.

The drying of air on screens

If there isn't a porch, you can lay the herb across screens that can be placed on your windows. You can hang them on the ceiling so that they get sun but not get out of the way. Air drying is the best option for herbs with low in moisture. This includes oregano, dill and rosemary.

Frame Drying

While drying your herbs frame-style takes a lot of time Many people believe it provides the best results overall. It's worth the effort and time they put into it. A lot of herbalists employ this method also, because they believe that the herbs retain the greatest effectiveness during the drying process.

In order to do this, you will need a box made of wood that measures 3 feet wide on all sides. The lid must be constructed out of glass. The bottom should be lined with foil and ensure that the lid is ventilated. Lay the herbs onto the foil, in one layer. Cover the lid with a secure ring and make sure to rotate every day until they're dry.

Set the frame in a spot where plants can receive plenty of sun every day. It is important to ensure that the box is waterproof in the event there is a nighttime rain. The rain could cause the plants to mold. It could take up to 6 weeks for this sort of drying of herbs to be completed.

Microwave

The most useful appliances you can use in your kitchen can be found in the microwave. It's definitely a fast and simple method of heating food items and freeze items that you want to cook. It is a great way to accelerate drying herbs?

The best way to accomplish this is to lay one piece of leaves that are dry on two sheets of paper towels. Make sure to use heavy-duty paper towels so they won't break. Place the paper towels as well as herbs in the microwave for two minutes at high. Let them fully cool.

Examine the herbs and if they're not completely dry, apply additional heat. 30 second increments are suggested to minimize the chance of burning. The duration however, will depend on the power of your microwave as well as the kind of plant material you're drying.

Oven Drying

When you've got a huge quantity of herbs to dry and dry, the microwave method could be slow. It is possible to speed up the process and have great results by the use of an oven. The herbs should be placed in one layer on the cookie sheet. The oven should be pre-heated to not greater than 200degF. Let the herbs remain inside the oven five minutes.

After they have completely cooled and cooled, they should be soft. If not, warm them in the oven for a second time, just a few minutes at each interval. Again, the kind of herb you choose to use will affect the time needed to get them dried.

Many people favor making use of the oven, or microwave method of drying because of the ease. You can dry herbs using these methods in just a few hours, versus weeks. This is particularly relevant for herbs with high moisture such as mint, chives and basil.

However, you should be extremely careful to ensure that you don't burn the plants. In the event that you cook them, or dry them too long, they're not going to be tasty or provide much nutritional value. Be aware that you don't want for the herbs to be cooked, but simply take out the moisture. Drying in the oven can reduce the strength of herbs by around one-third.

Dehydrator

It is possible to use a device called a dehydrator , which removes the moisture in your herbs. They range between $100-$400 based on the size, brand and the quality. It is a useful option when you have the money to purchase one.

When you use a dehydrator, you can control the temperature and effortlessly use the timer so you're never forgetting to check the temperature. They also circulate air, which is crucial for evenly drying herbs.

To get the most effective results, choose a dehydrator with a round shape. They are equipped with the ability to stack trays, which means you can place the herbs in layers on each tray and then dehydrate them at same at the same time. This will save you time and cuts down the drying time for all your herbs.

Salt Drying

Although salt drying isn't so popular than other techniques, it's nonetheless worthy of mention. It is possible to use table salt in order to dry the leaves. Put them in an oven tray, and sprinkle salt over them. It may take up to four weeks to dry in this manner.

Be sure to shake off the salt prior to packaging them. It is better to store the jars in glass instead of plastic bags If you've tried this method previously.

Freezing

You can also freeze your herbs. A lot of people who live in high-humidity regions utilize this method. The air's humidity is a major obstacle for them to make their plants sufficiently dry without aid of numerous heating options.

After the herbs have been cleaned then blanch them in boiling water. Let the herbs sit within the boiling water for a minute. Prepare a bowl of ice ready. Remove them as soon as you can out of the water that is boiling to an Ice bath.

Dry them off, pack the bags in freezer containers and store them. Make sure you get rid of the air before sealing them. Also, label the bag. The topic of labeling will be discussed in the following chapter.

Chapter 5: How To Store Dry Herbs

After your herbs have dried There's a final step to take: packaging them for appropriate storage. It's crucial not to lose the ball here otherwise all your efforts and time have been wasted.

It's a good idea to plan out the best place to store your dried herbs before you start. There isn't a lot of space, but you require a space that is dark and dry. It is also not advisable to keep them in the kitchen as they may absorb cooking oil and other odors that are strong.

Beware of storing them in the laundry room in case they be able to flavor and smell from dryer sheet. The basement, obviously is not a good alternative because of the humidity. If you reside in an area that has excessive humidity levels, you might have to consider running an air dehumidifier around your herbs as a safety measure.

Bags or Jars

There are those who disagree about using glass jars or baggies made of plastic to keep dried herbs. Both methods are employed and, in reality, there isn't any benefit to either one over either.

A lot of consumers love glass jars due to the fact that they allow you to recycle them. They are aware that glass won't cause harm to the environment. Use dark-colored glass whenever possible.

Other people appreciate the ease of bags, and they require less space to store. Bags are stackable easily.

It's all the individual's preference. Do not use metal containers because they may impart an metallic flavor. Beware of wooden containers as they take in moisture.

No matter which method you go about it, be sure your containers are in a sealed, airtight manner. For glass jars this implies lids that fit well. Make sure to secure them as tight as possible. When you have the bags in place, take out all air, and ensure that the closure is secure.

Labeling

Label your containers or bag of plants. This is vital since a lot of them may appear the same. The label you choose should contain:

* Sort of herb
* A part of the plant
* Date of packaging
* Drying method

Don't add any dried herb to a jar till it's gone completely. In the event that you do, the herbs might aren't as powerful as you would like or believed they were. After a few years they begin losing their potency.

If you're looking to store more herb, make a second container for it. Set this second jar on top of the first one to ensure you don't use it accidentally first. When the first jar has been used up you can then use the second container.

This is the exact type of revolving idea used by grocery stores for their goods. They shift the oldest product to the front , and then move the most recent items in the back. This method of rotation makes sure that certain items aren't left in the shelves for longer than other items.

Where can I store it?

It is important to keep the dried herbs in a safe place away from sunlight and water. Be sure to keep your herbs in the cellar or any other place where there is drafts or moisture. Do not store them in the kitchen because the odors from other foods could ruin them!

Do not store your herbs in a place that would allow a child or pet to access the herbs. Although they are safe to use but they could be hazardous when handled improperly. Certain herbs are extremely potent and can make the child or pet sick in the event of direct consumption. Pets and children are interested, and certain herbs are very fragrant!

If you'd like to display your herb garden but don't require any space. If your space is small you can consider an over-the-door shelf. It can be placed in a closet for hallways, for instance. The jars will fit on shelves and are simple to access. But they don't take up additional space within your home.

If you plan to store them in a freezer, it's an ideal idea to have an extra freezer independent from your normal one. Maybe your already own a huge freezer that is used to store meat and other things. You can make a separate section of it to your herb collection.

Examine the bags or jars you've packed and stored for a few days following the time you've done it. Examine them to ensure you didn't pack something with moisture inside. If you did, remove it out of the packaging or container and dry the contents once more. You can then repackage them.

If you don't inspect the contents, it could be disastrous later after opening the container or jar to discover the smell of mold and other issues. Set a reminder on your calendar to look them in the week following packaging. After that, you should check them every week following that. If you don't see any moisture-related signs then you're safe!

How long?

The majority of herbalists believe that it is possible to use herbs that are dried and stored for up to a year. After that, they diminish in potency and you shouldn't be relying on their effectiveness. There are people who have used them for up to 5 years after their packaging and reported positive outcomes, but it's an excellent chance to try.

Herbs can still be delicious for up to five years, and that's the reason why many people still use the herbs. However the potency of herbs decreases over time. The purpose of making use of herbs is to increase the value of nutrition and medicinal benefits. It is sensible to use herbs that are in the top quality.

It isn't a good idea to keep any over-the-counter or prescription medicines in your cupboard for five years, so avoid that for your herb products. This is the reason why the labeling aspect during the drying as well as packing procedure is vital!

If you realize that you're nearing the end of the year when you've not yet utilized all the benefits of a particular herb, you can find ways to utilize it. Find recipes that require it, and then try them! Your family and you will appreciate the change in your menu, since we are tired of the same meals over and over.

It is also possible to offer some of the herbs you have left to family members or friends during the final few days of the season. Maybe they haven't yet tried drying their own herbs yet but are curious. A taste test of their own could provide the motivation they'll must try at home! Also, sharing it with other people is better rather than throwing out any herbs that are not used.

Chapter 6: Common Mistakes To Avoid

When drying your herbs can be a learning experience, you shouldn't have to master certain skills by doing it the hard way. If you avoid these common mistakes, you'll benefit of your efforts and decrease the chance of rotting your herb.

#1--Using herbal remedies as a substitute to medical care.

Although you may use herbs for minor ailments, don't depend on them as a substitute for medical treatment. For instance, you might experience that the use of certain herbs can ease the discomfort and inflammation associated with your arthritis. However, you must maintain your regular appointments with your physician, however you must be open about the use of herbs.

It's fine to inform the doctor that you'd prefer to rely on these herbal remedies rather than taking prescription medication. This is your right but you should still to have annual checks and other medical treatments.

#2--Ignoring quality.

Be careful in the plant you pick. If they're not healthy and healthy, they will not be able to offer you medicinal or nutritional value. It's important to recognize that different plants are not identical.

Beginning with a growing herb plant instead of seeds -- is a popular method. Be sure to have examined the plants to make sure the health of them. If you spot any problems you should not to purchase them.

#3--Using chemicals.

Do not use chemicals or pesticides to aid your plants expand. The plants you want to be as natural as they can be. Only way to ensure this happen is to make sure that they're grown under the ideal conditions.

Utilize organic soil and natural methods to remove bugs and other creatures that can harm your plants. Make sure to regularly get rid of them and remove dead foliage frequently. If you let it persist, it could strip this healthy, healthy plant with the nutrition it requires to thrive.

#4 - Getting the wrong amount of light or water.

The proper amount of sunshine and water is crucial for herbs to flourish just as they should. The soil should be moist when you touch it , but not saturated. A lot of water could increase the likelihood of harmful bacteria and mold developing. Lack of water can cause a plant to be stunted.

The growth of herbs requires sunlight and thrive, so ensure you plant them on the windowsill or plant them outdoors in a place where they receive plenty. If you notice that certain herbs in your garden that are performing better than others, you can rotate the plants. The added sunlight is beneficial to them.

Do not plant outside in areas with excessive shade. Before planting, take note of the amount of sun and shade the area receives during the day. On days with higher temperatures your plants could need more water than normal So, pay attention to the way they perform in different weather conditions.

#5--Overcrowding.

Make sure your plants have plenty of space to expand. They don't just get taller, but they require to expand too. Insufficient conditions can cause plants to become weak or sick, since it adapts to the environment it's given. For well-groomed plants, you will see less better and you'll be able to have the highest yield from this particular herb.

#6--Seeding.

If you trim and harvest your plants regularly and regularly, they will not seed. Seeding is the sign of the conclusion of the growth. By cutting and pruning your plants, you allow them to continue growing. This will prolong the cycle of growing them and harvesting the plants.

#7--Don't dry the herbs completely.

One of the biggest mistakes when drying herbs is that you don't dry them completely. Be patient with any drying method and make sure they are dry. Be sure to test for dryness after a few days after packaging. If they're not dry, now is the moment to remove them and dry them out more.

#8: Not packing them correctly.

Don't let yourself be sloppy when it comes to the final step of packaging. You must label your herbs so that you know the type of herb they are and how long they've been in your home. Use airtight bags , or airtight containers. Protect your storage from sunlight and moist.

#9--Not knowing about your specific herb.

It's a major mistake not to know about the specific herbs you will be growing. The more you understand about the best methods to grow and harvesting methods drying techniques and so on. The more simple it will be.

This is the reason why you should start with a couple of herbs initially. Once you've become more proficient in the process it is possible to consider adding more plants to your garden. A lot all at once could make you feel overwhelmed.

#10--Running the procedure.

Even though your days are extremely busy, you should make some time to start. The first steps are the most time-consuming. It's then an issue of keeping them hydrated and making sure they receive enough sunlight.

Take note of the times when your herbs require to be cut back, too. If you do not pay attention to this it can hinder growth and reduce the quality of your herbs.

Make sure you have enough time to harvest as well as drying. The plants won't follow your schedule, therefore you need to be prepared for them. It is essential to allow drying all the time it needs and shouldn't be completed in a hurry.

#11--I'm not even trying.

Refusing to give up before you start is a guarantee of failure! Many people believe they're not capable of doing this, which is why they never even attempt. But, if you follow the steps step-by step and following the steps you'll achieve results.

You can cultivate the herbs you want, dry them, and then to have them available at any time you'd like. Utilize the information you've learned in this book to help begin your journey. You deserve credit for moving forward and testing. Find out what works for

you, and then create an action plan to keep
you on track.

Chapter 7: The General Herbs To Dry

There are way too many plants to mention them all However, you can dry anything you want to make use of. Here's a list the most commonly used herbs you can consider drying. There are no one right or wrong type to use. Take a look at what you are looking for from a nutritional perspective and work from there.

Antioxidants

One of the main reasons why that people take herbs is due to the potent antioxidants that they provide. They help eliminate free radicals and toxins from your body. In the end, you'll be healthier both inside and outside.

The plants that provide the highest antioxidant levels are:

* Allspice
* Cloves
* Cinnamon
* Lemon Balm
* Marjoram

* Oregano

* Peppermint

* Rosemary

* Saffron

* Thyme

Additional Benefits

There are some plants you could dry and use to gain specific advantages. Once you have learned about the benefits it might inspire you to plant and harvest these plants. Here's a list effects that could be of interest to you.

You'll have healthier and younger looking skin.

A lot of people are searching for an answer to the question of how young they are! They do not want to see wrinkles, wrinkles and lines when they glance at themselves in the mirror. The protection of your skin cells is essential to keep you looking natural.

Italian spices are often added to the food that you cook. Basil is probably the most well-known Italian spice in cooking. It not only tastes delicious however, it can also help to safeguard skin cells. The potent antioxidants in basil may also aid your body fight harmful bacteria.

Basil helps to reduce the risk of having serious health issues. This includes Alzheimer's, various kinds of cancers as well as heart disease and osteoporosis. All of these are health issues which can affect your overall quality of life, which is why combating them is crucial.

Encourage Healing

As we age as we age, it may take your body longer to heal cuts. This could increase the risk of developing bacterial infections. In the body, harmful bacteria can cause Sore throat or strep throat or even pneumonia in the course of.

Thyme is a potent herb which can aid in healing. It fights harmful bacteria, but doesn't kill the beneficial bacteria that reside in your body. Thyme is also able to alleviate throat pain and inflammation. It aids the body in healing scrapes and cuts quicker.

Reduce Inflammation

For many people chronic pain is a an everyday occurrence. But, it can limit their mobility and their quality of life in many ways. Sage is a plant which can aid in reducing inflammation as well as reduce the ageing process of the body.

The inflammation that is caused by this is typically caused by asthma, different forms of arthritis, as well as the hardening of the arteries. Incorporating sage into the meals you eat frequently can be a healthy method to reduce pain and inflammation that comes with these ailments.

Sleep More Soundly

If your body is able rest comfortably, you'll be amazed at how much happier you feel. Your body and mind require rest to be refreshed and relaxed. The constant twitching and turning throughout the night can make you feel uncomfortable at the start of the day.

Utilizing sleep aids may make you feel groggy and drowsy in the morning. Marjoram is one herb that naturally helps you sleep more easily and longer.

Marjoram is most effective in the form of an extract. It's very potent therefore you'd only require approximately 5 drops of the oil in the bath. Begin taking it before bed and observe how your mood improves at the start of your day!

Boost Your Immune System

Prevention is an integral element of a healthy life. Don't wait until you do not feel well enough to act. Oregano is a great herb to look into if want to improve your immunity. It may help lower the chance of developing health issues from bacteria, viruses and free radicals. Oregano is frequently utilized to treat infections with natural antimicrobial, and an anti-fungal natural ingredient. It is a great way to clear an infection of yeast or nail fungus problem.

Maintain Heart Health

Healthy heart health is vital at any age, however, it becomes more vital as we age. The heart disease has been the main cause of death for women and men within the USA. Ginger is an excellent option for lessening the risk of heart disease.

Ginger has been found to reduce the chance of arteries that are blocked. This is an important element in the prevention of heart attacks. Ginger can also help to prevent the occurrence of fungus and other bacteria from infecting the heart. It also improves immunity. Additionally it is an effective approach to lower good cholesterol, also known as LDL.

Improve Digestion

If your body isn't digesting food properly, it could make you feel very uncomfortable. It is possible to experience gas, acid reflux or constipation. All of these symptoms aren't pleasant. Allspice is a distinctive flavor which is extremely delicious as it can be put into many food items or even used in tea.

This herb can be used to boost digestion overall. It can also help the digestive tract. It can help with acid problems because it improves digestion. It is possible to add allspice to your meals, vegetables soups, and broths.

Allspice is also a great way in regulating the blood sugar level. It's helpful for managing cholesterol too. It provides a lot of flavor to your meals, and it also has a lot of value for general health.

Combat Bacteria

If we could detect bacteria and germs everywhere the place, it could be a complete nightmare. We depend on our immune system to keep us as healthy as is possible. Cinnamon can help fight harmful bacteria. It could even help stop serious health issues which would require antibiotics or other powerful treatments.

The joints and muscles of our bodies may begin to become smaller and less flexible as we older. Cinnamon may help reduce these issues, since it is a natural anti-inflammatory ingredient. It also reduces the dangers of gum diseases, E. bacteria, as well as infections of the urinary tract (UTIs).

Prevention of Cancer

The fight against cancer is a serious one and can cost many lives. The prevention of cancer should be top on your priority list when taking good care of yourself. Turmeric is an amazing plant that will help you accomplish this. It can also help lower the risk of developing Alzheimer's disease.

Turmeric contains curcumin, which is the ingredient that provides the roots with its yellow color. Curcumin assists in preventing DNA mutations that can cause cancer.

Create a healthier mind and Body

It appears that the most powerful herb is the clove. It's extremely potent due to a myriad of reasons. It helps reduce the pain of joints and muscles and is packed with powerful antioxidants that boost your immune system and combat free radicals.

Eugenol is present in cloves that are a form of natural and mild anesthesia. It can help ease the pain of irritation of the throat, sore gums or toothache. Cloves may also provide relief to people suffering from breathing problems such as asthma and bronchitis.

Cloves are a well-known antibacterial and anti-fungal remedy, too. In fact, you cannot go wrong with application of cloves. There's so much it can shield you from!

Chapter 8: How To Prepare To Dry Herbs

The process of drying spices can be described as a procedure that demands a lot of preparation as anything else you'll do. You don't want to buy a large quantity of spices you

You shouldn't use them unless you're prepared to dry the items. This doesn't mean that you should not be used, unless you are prepared to dry them.

If you are still slacking off drying your favorite spices. The methods are easy and quick to implement and dry your spices whenever you'd like

Select the method you wish to apply

There are many methods that you can employ to dry your spice. Certain methods like air drying are easy and practical. But air drying isn't appropriate for certain climates or environments. Drying using the microwave will hold the shade and type of spices, while drying in a dehydrator will require that you purchase the equipment or create one by using cardboards or compressed wood. The microwave drying method is ideal for the spices with low dampness, such as Parsley, Rosemary, Marjoram, Oregano, and Dill. Herbs with a lot of moisture like Basil, Mint and Chives are best dried in dehydrators or in the oven.

Harvest the herbs

You can harvest your spices anytime, but the most effective time to harvest them is early in the morning, after the dew has dried off the leaves. It is recommended to collect your spices prior to the blooming in the event that you have to pick flowers. Assuming you've been reaping your herbs regularly however, your plants may not have had the opportunity of blossoming, and you could collect and dry them at any time. Typically the non-tough spices start diminishing as the weather gets cooler, which is why it's better to collect and dry them out in the late the summer.

To preserve the majority of the flavor, chop spices early in the morning, right once the dawn dew is dry,. However, do not wait until the ferocity from the sun is drying the

Ointments. You'll want these strong revitalizing balms, so plan your gathering well. It's also a good idea to select the plants early, before they start becoming wilted due to the sun's evening rays

To collect, chop the branches that are solid and comes from the plants you are planning to dry. Get rid of all dry, infected, and spotted and shriveled leaves. Leaves with a yellow hue and those that have spots, may be harmful, so you shouldn't want dried them. These kinds of spice can be used to

Have slowed down.

Take off all lower leaves, which measure around 1 inch away from the branch. Take the stems or branches using your hands, and gently shake them until any crawlies or insects that grip them will fall off or break off. Get rid of any soil prior to when you begin drying.

If you have picked your spices by taking the plants, then shake the soil off.

Certain plants require cleaning therefore you must rinse them in cool water. Then, wipe the dirt with soft air towels. Cleanse the spices by applying cool water in colander. It is possible to use a mixed greens plate and a spinner for drying the spice in case you own one. Don't dry everything at once, but dry only a few at one time. In the event that you don't own an assortment of mixed greens spinner apply the herbs to several layers of newspaper towels to take out as much water as you can particularly if you're using microwaves or ovens to dry them, otherwise they'll get dried out due to the moisture and not dry.

Herb leaves must be picked when the natural ointments present in the plants are the most notable. The fragrant spices such as Basil Chervil, Marjoram and Savory are able to be harvested prior to their bloom. Many spices, including Basil, Coriander, Cilantro, Lemon salve, Mint Parsley, Rosemary, and Sage can be cut during the growth season.

Bunch drying

This is a straightforward method to dry a variety of spices with long stems like Basil, Sage, Mint, Parsley, Dill, Marjoram, Rosemary and Savory in addition to many others.

If your leaves are spotless You can dry them out without washing them to keep the oils from escaping during flushing. However If the spices appear filthy or dusty, then it is recommended to flush them gently with cool water. Shake the spices to remove excess water, and then tie them into small bundles to hang.

Secure 4 - 6-branches or 5--10 branches according to their size, and join them in a group. You can tie them with a string, thread, or the rubber band. A rubber band is preferred since the bundles will continue shrinking when they dry, while the band can adapt. Be sure to check every now and then to ensure that the herbs aren't falling out and make sure to tighten the band. You can tie smaller bundles if drying spices that have high levels of dampness.

Place the herbs in a place where that the water will evaporate.

Bring the herb bundles inside and hang them upside-down by putting the leaves facing upwards and the leafy ends facing down. Put them in a dry, warm location with adequate air circulation. Pick a place that is well-ventilated and doesn't get direct sunlight.

The upside-down hanging of herbs ensures that essential oils present in the stems are absorbed into the leaves. Do not hang them in a hot surface, such as above the stove as the heat and odors can affect the taste the texture, aroma, and flavor.

To keep dust from accumulating on the dried leaves Place each bunch in an airtight bag prior to hanging. Then, gather the top of the bag, and secure it with a knot, so the leaves hang free. To let air circulate, make holes into the bag.

Label each bag of paper by the herb's name as well as the date.

Place the herb bundles upside down, so that the leaves are facing downwards within the bags. Be sure the herbs do not get clogged in the bag, so that they will have enough airflow to dry out and prevent becoming moldy or rotting. The proper circulation of air is important since wet herbs can develop mold and begin to rot.

Be sure to check regularly to determine the extent to which they are drying, and ensure that you check them until they're completely dry and ready to be stored.

Tray drying

Trays are commonly used in households to dry seed as well as massive leaves of spices. This is an easy method to dry spices outdoors or inside. It's great for spice that have short stems and aren't able to use to hang.

The shallow-rimmed plates are usually great and you can also cover the spice with cheesecloth.

Drying leaves

Take the leaves off the stems, or dry them off on their stems. Spread a layer of leaves on the tray to allow them to dry quickly and there will be sufficient air circulation.

Place the tray containing the stems or leaves in a dry, warm area that is well-ventilated. Avoid exposing the plants to direct sunlight as this can accelerate drying.

The leaves should be turned over each day, but do it gently to ensure that they aren't crushed when they dry. Drying takes about one week or two, however it is contingent on the amount of moisture in the plant and the temperature and humidity of the location at the moment. Be sure to let the herbs dry completely prior to storing the herbs.

If the leaves are crispy and dry completely, place their contents in an airtight sealed container.

Drying seeds

After harvesting your seeds distribute them across tray sheets as thin sheets.

The same procedure should be followed as you followed for drying the leaves.

Check that they are dry. Rub them between your fingers and blow them away gently.

The seeds should be stored within airtight containers.

There are several methods you can employ to dry spices to use in the kitchen as flavors and flavorings like we'll discover in Chapter 4.

Things You Might Be In Need of

The drying of spices using paper is an option which is used by a lot of people in the present. It's not yet a viable option however you must be on the lookout for your spices to avoid the development of mold when plants don't receive enough wind flow. Continue turning the spices so that they dry across all sides. The traditional method for drying plants using screens can also be employed for drying spices. Old window screens can useful, especially if they are placed on blocks that allow the wind to pass through all bearings. In the event that you're using papers or screens, keep them away from the breeze to protect them from moving them around as they dry and turn light.

Dehydrator

A drying out device or dehydrator can be used to help evaporate spices and accelerate the drying process. This helps in the process, particularly in the event that you have a huge of. You can dry many spices at once if you are making use of the right equipment.

dehydrator. It's also useful as you can place spices in it as you eat. Spices that are dried in a dehydrator usually retain their colour and quality especially when dried at low temperatures. Always check the plates inside the stack for any indication that they are damp, and revise the plates to ensure that air is controlled.

There are a variety of dehydrators on the market that come with all the features you need. Some include fans, indoor regulators plates that are washable and removable and other features. Choose a model that is approved for use at home and ensure that the plates are washable and easy to clean. Choose one that is suitable for the space you'll need to store it in, which is likely in the kitchen, or somewhere else.

Cheesecloth

Cheesecloth could give the impression of something that is clear in the kitchen. However, despite its simplicity, it's simple, it's extremely useful. It really helps when cooking, making preparations or drying your spices. Layer cheesecloth on the plants as they dry remove spices from their oils, and make bouquets garni during cooking, or for other tasks. The cheesecloths that are tightly woven can be more expensive, however they're more effective when you layer them to create channels. It is easier to layer less of cheesecloth that is good quality when you are segregating. However you don't have to spend much on them because you'll require some within your home kitchen.

Scales

When you are making or improving food, you will add flavors and flavor here and there, however there are times when that your recipe requires precise estimations. You can invest your resources in the form of an Electronic kitchen scale that can quantify your ingredients as you require. The majority of kitchen scales aren't expensive, but you should look for the most essential features without regard to cost.

Things to look out for:

The most basic scales will include at least American as well as Metric digital measurements. This is usually found in the most basic scales.

A Tare feature eliminates any weight from measurements, allowing you to measure only the herbs that are added.

The scale should be simple to remove. Glass is superior as well than other, non-reactive substances.

They are, in addition, an essential kitchen appliances, which you can use to harvest dry and keep your seasonings and spices.

Tips on HARVESTING a variety of parts of HERBAL PLANTS

There are many ways to make spices, whether in pots or your garden at home, or obtain some from a friend or a friend. It is essential to understand the components you can harvest due to the fact that you might need to harvest them, in order to understand why. Spices are best harvested when you have the ideal time to reap them. the timings differ based on the specific plant part you want to harvest.

The next step is to establish guidelines you must be aware of when collecting each part of a plant in order to reap the maximum benefits from your cooking flavors and seasonings.

Leaves

The majority of us utilize herbal leaves in our kitchens to enhance the flavor of food, whether it's stew, meat soups, sauces, soups and salads, in addition to other food items. It is typical to find dried or fresh herbs in the majority of kitchens. Herbal leaves are utilized for cooking and to season food items. Some are used as preservatives , and others are used for medicinal reasons. It is crucial to harvest these herbs prior to when they have lost their essential oils. The best time to harvest leaves so that they will retain their essential oils is in the morning hours when the leaves are dry. The leaves of herbs that are picked at the right moment are extremely healthy and comprise the majority of flavouring and medicinal components.

The fresh leaves are available at any time of the year throughout the development of the spice. The majority of them are used immediately after gathering, and are used in planning or to arrange of teas that are new. But what do you do with the extra leaves? Dry them. When you collect your own leaves from your plant nursery to dry them, make sure that you collect them towards the morning after the dew is dry. This should be done before the sun has begun to blister to keep the oils that are medicinal. As soon as the sun heats the plants to a high degree the oils that help rejuvenate the plant disappear. The perfect time to reap ensures that most of oils that rejuvenate are retained in the leaves.

Take the leaves in the spring when they are still young prior to the blooming of the plant. It is best to collect young at the time the plant is at its phase of development due to the fact that this

This is the time when the leaves are the most affluent of their flavor. For evergreen spices such as Rosemary and Thyme the leaves may be picked up shortly before they begin blooming to take on the majority the flavor.

It is also important to collect as often as you can. You could even gift your loved ones dried spices for gifts.

Whole Plants

If you have to harvest the entire plant of spices or flying pieces with or without roots, the optimal time to collect the parts is long before the plant begins to bloom. When you realize it is about to flower, you can cut off the entire stem or take the entire plant out depending on whether you truly want the leaves. In the moment the plant is unable to fill again in many instances thus it will be able to contain the majority of the supplementation as it would have required their development for the re-development. If you plan to gather wild spices and you're really looking to dry the whole plant, you must try as much as you can reasonably be expected to harvest less than 33 percent in the entire plant.

Flowers

Flowers are generally extremely sensitive so you must pick the flowers with caution. The most ideal time to harvest blossoms is late in the morning, as they're dry. However, do not pick them up when they're wet. The blossoms begin to fade when it's hot. They could even become spoiled when you pick them during a hot summer day. If you place them in a container, when you're reaping them, they'll stack up over each other and then get extremely warm. Be sure not to store their holder. While picking the blossoms make sure you avoid all of them which have any damage spots, rot, or spots. Don't pick blossoms which have fallen from the plant as they need be fresh and ready to use. Once you've completed the process of picking themup, bring them into the home and take them out of the holder for collecting or crate. Bring your picks to the dry location whenever time permits. This will protect the blossoms from swelling. Handle flowers with care to be safe from damage.

Fruits and Seeds

Seeds are harvested with perseverance because you must wait until they're fully developed. It is best to wait until the organic ingredients are in place and the plants grow into adults before you can begin collecting seeds. The ideal day to gather is when the seeds are dry, but in a short time, the seeds begin to scatter. Be sure to check that the seeds are not turning green. Once they turn brown or dark this is the time when you know they are ready to be collected. The signs of preparation are the time when

organic products have matured, or when the seeds are contained in the unit are dry. Seeds that have been prepared are typically well-solidified, and often they are dry pods.

Don't harvest too early and don't gather until you've reached the point of no return. If you harvest too soon, the seeds haven't been prepared and could take shape or begin to decay once they dry. If you harvest past the point of no return, you'll lose the largest part of the seeds , which are been scattered. This is why you have to be alert to be aware of the best chance. The natural products need drying will get older and turn yellow, red, and brown with shading in different shades.

Roots

The most ideal time to harvest home-grown roots is during the fall although some groundskeepers also take them up in the spring. It is during this time that the roots that are grown at home are in good shape to be harvested. From all the parts that are grown at home of the plant it is the roots that are most striking, but you'll need to put in a lot of effort to get rid of some although not all varieties are easy to harvest. This could be one of the reasons why a lot of people don't dry the roots they grow at home, however they're so healthy. Many organic roots may be removed by exposing hands, especially those with small hands. Retrieving roots that have created a solid base in the soil, is laborious work.

You will be able to reap many benefits from them. They are flavorings, natural teas , and combinations of different jobs. Eliminating them requires certain responsibility from you but there are simple ways to ease the process.

Important Tips:

The most efficient way to harvest roots is to discover the entire root system. You should be careful when you burrow. It is possible to slacken the roots by using your cultivating spade. Press and lift the entire base of the plant and around it so that the whole root structure can be lifted up. This is the primary way you can remove roots that grow quickly and also those that grow deeper into the soil. Get rid of the roots you have to pull and place them in the back and then replant the rest to continue growth. You can collect only what you want by separating the root structure. Make sure you do not leave gaps that are expanding. Top them off with soil.

Some roots are able to solidify that they solidify a lot when they dry. This is why it's ideal to strip, wash and cut them while they're still young. At this point, they're fragile, in any event. If they dry. This will make be unable to work with them in the event you didn't strip or cut into smaller pieces. The dried roots may be so strong enough that it's hard to crush them completely. They'll look like rocks once they're totally dried. They should be cleaned thoroughly and then wash the soil in the event that you're really keen to. Peel them and cut them off as you are able to.

Bark

The herbaceous bark (i.e. cinnamon) is used to enhance the flavor of food items and you can either utilize the sticks to flavor your food or grind them into powder. The process of harvesting bark could result in the plant to suffer damage, therefore you must take care to do it right so that you will have her for a long period of time. Don't cut the bark off around the entire tree in or in any other way that it could not continue to grow. If you do then you'll be removing the source of food that helps the tree in its development and could cause it to turn dry and slow its growth. Reap only a small amount of each time, and don't force its growth.

The methods used to dry HERBS

Drying and growing spices is among the easiest ways to preserve food. The majority of spices have little moisture which makes it easier to keep them safe after collecting. Drying your own spices and flavor is sensible considering the substantial cost of flavors and flavors. When you create yourself, you will realize that you're acquiring new and organic flavors and flavors. You may also create your favorite spices and select the ones you enjoy.

Air-Drying

You can tie the branches together by tying them with the help of a string or rubber band. Smaller bundles are simpler to dry and dry faster than larger ones. Place the herb bundle and with their stems facing forward in a bag of paper or wrap the leaves around flowers. Secure the ends of the bag in order to seal it making sure you

Don't take care not to crush the herbs. Be sure to poke a few holes into the bag to allow for air ventilation. Place the bag in a cool and well-ventilated area as described earlier. Be sure the stems are hung upside down to ensure that the vital oils are retained. So, the essential oils will move through the leaves. The spices may be dry and ready to be stored within one week or so.

Plants drying in the sunlight or in the outdoors

Many people prefer not to use this method due to the fact that plants are faded and go through the loss of the majority of flavors and oils. People who prefer this method use it to dry blossoms and leaves to make for purposes.

Cut the plants once they have dried. Join them together using elastic groups. Use similar sizes to ensure drying will be consistent. Hang plants confronting downward.

Make use of the garden to hang them, or use an organizer and hang them wherever there is enough light. Let them dry for a significant amount of time until they dry and then check them regularly. Secure the plants due to the winds.

Take them out as the blossoms and leaves get crisp. Drying plants in the indoors

For drying spices in the air, It is important to remove the plants once it's dry. You

Dry the stems and blossoms by tying them into packs and hanging them upside down. It is best to do this placed in a dry and warm location, but you should keep away from the kitchen, and any steam-producing sources. In the kitchen , there are cooking fumesthat can affect drying.

Connect the packs using turn tie, elastic groups or even a small amount of wire that you will be able to switch out if the need arises. When the flowers or stems start drying, they require the string or wire to be secured to keep them in place as they restrain when they dry.

The bundles can be wrapped using:

Muslin

An mesh bag for produce

A paper bag that has numerous holes. The bag must be tied around the neck.

It's possible to dry the flowers or leaves independent of each other, which means you'll need to put them in somewhere to dry. Drying screens, lattice, old window screens, or other are all suitable for use. Lattices must be stapled or nail to the edge of a wooden board to keep drying plants getting in contact with dirty surfaces. Cheesecloth can be used to cover a sub-par area drying your flowers and then, after that, place them in a single layer to ensure they dry properly.

Drying can occur at any point between hours and days. Once you are sure that your spices are dry, place your spices inside dry containers as well as containers.

Solar Drying

Not all climates are suitable for sun-oriented drying. This will require a warm, dry climate with an average temperature of 100 degrees. The moisture should be at least 60 degrees or less. If these conditions are in place you may use the heat of solar radiation to dry out your spice in a normal manner. But, it is not recommended to expose the spices to lots of direct sunlight as they could lose balms that help rejuvenate and result in bleaching.

The process of solar drying includes:

Place the plants on drying mesh or screens, outside until they begin to become tough before transferring them inside to rest during the night.

Drying the herbs on the rear or windshield in your car on hot days.

It is possible to dry them using a solar-powered food dehydrator that is possible to construct. You can place drying screens in the device, which can be placed one on top of one to permit drying different herbs simultaneously. The food dehydrator comes with a glass-topped top to absorb radiation. Install an absorber to transfer the heat of sunlight to plants. Install a vent that allows the air to circulate so that the plants don't suffer from mold.

The advantage of this technique is that it's the most typical method and is also affordable. You are also able to dry as many spices you like. The disadvantage of sun-powered drying, is the fact that not all regions are able to enjoy the ferocity of the sun's arrival with a temperature of 100°. Certain regions are less heat, while other areas get more. Additionally, you may have drying your ingredients and tastes at various times, but not necessarily in the summer months. The moisture test is also a good one across a variety of locations.

Drying in the refrigerator

Another method you can employ in drying spices is put them in an ice box and let them sit in there. This may seem like neglect, but it's not. You may have noticed that when you placed the spices on the edges they'll dry on their own. This could take just two days, depending on the type of herbs.

However, you must keep them out of bundling in or any other method that could cause them to cause them to spoil. The spices should be left open, and the dryness and cold that the colder provides will allow them to dry up until they're solid. They also retain their flavor, color and smell making this the best method of drying some herbs.

This method was used to dry Chives and Parsley that retain their unique flavor when dried unlike the other methods used. The primary challenge that occurs when you employ this method is trying to locate enough space in your refrigerator to dry all the spices that you'll need. If you've got extra space in the fridge, dry some spices , particularly those that have lost the flavor easily. You can put a few of your spice in your refrigerator and leave them out for a few days. Then, add more as space allows. If your refrigerator is limited space, dry other spices elsewhere or dry them in their sections. Once the main parcel is dry put them in a storage container and keep them in the refrigerator. Drying in the oven

It is possible to think that drying spices and other flavors within the oven is straightforward but it's not. You may have tried it in the past and even if you've tried as so, you'll realize that the work has increased and requires a lot of energy. To allow spices and flavors to fully dry it is recommended to dry them at around 100°F, but in fact, a lot of stoves cannot be set to that temperature. The spices require airflow which can be a challenge as there are stoves that don't have vents.

If you decide to make use of your oven to dry herbs, you'll require an oven thermometer to gauge the heat and use it to test this method. You'll need to turn the oven down to its lowest setting, i.e. warm, and then turning off for a period of time. At the same time you must keep the oven's lighting on to monitor the herbs and decide whether they require more or less.

Method:

They can also be dried using the oven and can be used to be used for both medicinal and culinary uses.

Set the oven at a low temperature. The lowest temperature it can be. Open the door.

Place the herbs on a baking tray and put it on the lower part of the oven. Spread cheesecloth over a wire cooling rack, and layer the herbs on the top. This will allow air circulation to be created all over. Set the rack and scattered herbs in the oven in the middle of the oven when temperatures are around 100 degrees.

Let the herbs dry, but continue to turn the herbs over frequently.

Herbs dry out much more quickly when cooked than vegetables and fruits. They dry quickly and do not spoil easily. If you're looking to play with drying in the oven, begin drying herbs prior to drying vegetables and fruits. Drying food items with the help of ovens can prove challenging and you must start with herbs.

It is possible to open the oven just a bit and test the temperature using your thermometer to ensure that it's at or near 100 degrees. Lower the temperature settings if it's higher than that or turn off for a few minutes.

The advantage of this method is that the majority of households have broilers so it is possible to dry spices as well as other flavors quicklyand at any point.

It is a disservice to say that this is not the most effective approach. Also, it's not cost effective because of the energy required.

Microwave Drying

It is possible to use the microwave for drying your spice but it's not recommended for drying foods with a lot of moisture. Drying spices and other flavors using this method may not be as easy than drying them with solar-powered drying or electric dehydrators, but it is possible to use it to dry spice varieties that are dry. Method:

Take off any diseased, spotted or discolored leaves. Take the leaves off the stems, then wash them. Lay them between the layers of paper towels.

Layer the sheets over the herbs. Make sure the herbs contained in the towels aren't excessively large. Lay other towels over the herbs.

Place the herbs in the microwave and turn the temperature to the HIGH setting. Dry them for around 2 minutes, but this is contingent on the type of herb you're drying.

Take a look every few seconds i.e. 30 seconds to ensure that they're not burned.

Place the microwave on high for 1 minute in the event that the herbs are hard. Then let them sit for 30 seconds. The drying process should be alternated between 30 seconds of the highest power, and then 30 second of rest. The majority of herbs will dry in 10 minutes or less time.

Take the paper towel off from the oven and allow the herbs to rest for a few minutes. The moisture that was absorbed by in the microwave evaporates into air. Set them on a wire rack or lay them out on a clean material , and let them cool.

Keep your herbs stored in airtight jars or containers. Make sure that the herbs are protected from heat and light. You can also seal airtight bags.

The advantage of this technique is that it's simple and fast. It also helps preserve the flavor and color which makes it very extremely popular.

The key is to be aware in all instances that you could end up cooking the spices and igniting the fire if you're not cautious.

Machine Dehydrating

Food dehydrators come in various sizes, and prices range from low to expensive. If you do not harvest tons of plants to dry, pick an appropriate machine to meet your needs. Place it in a suitable location in which you can dry your flavors and flavor without having to contend with your machine's capacity.

Drying using this device is straightforward because it comes with the ability to use indoor clocks, regulators and regulators. Certain people also layer plant material on the plates and let them dry, without turning on the machine.

A lot of dehydrators regulate the temperature and are able to change it whenever you need to. They also come with a fan that circulates the air. There are round models as well as boxes that are fitted with various stacking plates that are washable. It is also possible to use them to seal batters for baking buns and bread and also to refine your yogurt. Follow the manufacturer's instructions to ensure that your machine is in top condition.

HOW TO Dry and store your herbs

After reaping, it is necessary to dry the spice and store for a period of time. In this section , you'll discover how you can dry and store every part of the plant you've harvested. You can also purchase brand new spice and store them after of using the spices you like. This ensures you have a ready inventory when you are required to use flavorings and seasonings.

Drying leaves

When you think about drying spices and flavor The first aspect you consider would be drying the leaves. Leaves are typically the first part of a spice most of us think about drying. Leaves are employed in the preparation for a wide variety of teas, herbal teas and food preparation plans. They also are used in a variety of home-grown dishes. It is important to handle the leaves to preserve their taste and color as the surface. Naturally, you shouldn't require squashed leaves if you desire embellishment of the entire leaf. Avoid the growth of mold and buildup on leaves because they're not beneficial. Get rid of these leaves, and this is good for your health.

To properly dry your leaves, you must dry them completely. Reap them, with or without stems after the dew is dry, but before it gets to be too hot out. You can keep these leaves outdoors or in the house, but away from direct sunlight as you select them. This will help to keep the ointments for rejuvenation inside the plant and prevent from speeding drying. If you believe that the spices are in good condition, it might not be necessary to wash them. They require a quick shake to remove any remaining dirt and insects. This is all you'll need to do and you can begin drying the spices. It is possible to dry the leaves of spices in tiny packages, joining the stems together with string or a band that is flexible. It is possible to use flexible material, so that it will change in the same way that spices psychologists do to stop the leaves from falling. The stems will certainly provide psychology when they dry because of dehydration.

It is also possible to use paper bags to cover the natural groups. It is recommended to wrap the spices in sacks of paper before you tie them. The sacks of paper protect the spices from the effects of light and particles of residue. Additionally, dried leaves, that tumble off the stems are sucked up and in a clinched. This is especially true for smaller leaves like Thyme leaves, that are trapped within the bags of paper rather than falling. A drying out machine or dehydrator could be

It is used to dry natural leaves. This helps make the process faster, cutting the amount of time needed to dry the spices completely. The leaves that you grow yourself in the dehydrator with low temperatures retain their green hue for a significant amount of the time. Even Basil retains its hue when you dry it at lower temperatures inside a dehydrator equipped with an air-flow fan. Or, you can flip the leaves often in the absence of a fan. It is possible to dry leaves on paper or screens.

Drying Flowers

Herb flowers are extremely delicate and require a delicate touch. The dried flowers can function the same way as the leaves of a spice plant, however treated with the least strain of care, since expanding or breaking the petals can cause rot to grow. Herbal flowers that are properly dried will keep their shade and scent. In the event that only the petals are needed, I believe that it's easier to allow the flower head to dry over a period of time then remove the petals in order to finish drying. The blossoms will have an opportunity for the petals to soften so that they are easier to remove. Drying Seeds

Keep those spice seeds that you collect from one season to the next. Because most spice seeds are organic and non-GMO-based, you are saving the most suitable seeds for your growing area.

To dry the spice seeds remove the seeds' heads and allow them to dry in one layer. Paper is a great choice to accomplish this. Beware of anything that can create the slightest breeze while drying seeds. There's nothing more painful than a mid-year storm that blows your dill reap across the floor of your stable. I'm speaking from personal experience.

Seeds dry quickly within two or three weeks. There is no way to cover dry seeds for a long period of time. I usually dry them sufficiently to rub the seeds off the head of the seed, then I place them in containers made of bricklayer with the cover of muslin for a month to allow any dampness that could remain, to evaporate. Then, I close the jar, and store it in a dark, cool area until required.

Drying Roots

Herbal roots are loaded with benefits for health, and can be extremely beneficial for us. But, they're not dried regularly as flowers and leaves are. The roots that are grown at home are healthy and nutritious and ought be dried in order to ensure they are available at all times. Even though that you could want to make use of fresh home grown roots, it is best to dry these precious plants.

Before drying, the roots need to be thoroughly cleaned. The removal of soil and other residues from the root can be difficult due to the amount of time they've spent in dirt. Use a vegetable-based cleaning brush to scrub away all soil that is stuck in the root. Make sure to use a lot of water while cleaning, and then remove the hairs on your roots before you begin the process of getting.

Clean up any soil that has accumulated while the root is drying.

Attaches should be removed before they have dried, and that's the time when they're still fresh like Marshmallow. They must be stripped first because it's hard to remove them once they have dried. There are some roots, like Comfrey that are just too big to grind, especially on a coffee maker at home. It is necessary cut these roots down to smaller sizes, which is appropriate when they're fresh. After the roots have dried, it is much more difficult crushing them down into powder. It's a lot harder to crush them in the event that your home espresso machine is equipped with a blade made of plastic.

Cut the roots and dry them in a single layer to keep them from mold. The process can be made easier by drying each one of the base layers using the dehydrator. This ensures that your flavor and flavors will be free of dampness. In any event, you can dry them with different methods and they'll dry even on paper and screens however, you'll need to carefully screen them.

How to Store Dry Herbs

Storing spices is a fantastic method of protecting them so that you can utilize them in the future. The storage of spices in dried form is an established method to safeguard spices and is easy and worth the effort. You can use dried spices straight from containers or compartments as you need to use them. You can use them to add flavor to your chicken, meat stew, fish soup, stew, and various food types while cooking or decorating your meals with these spices and tastes. They can be used in your sauces as well as mixed greens. They are available in many varieties shades, colors and flavors that add flavor to food and create a delicious and appealing taste.

Certain spices, like Mint Thyme, Marjoram, Oregano and Rosemary dry well. The dried spice can be used in the same way as you would new spices, but you would like lesser amounts of money because they require more considered. But, you must dry them with the proper methods to preserve their colors, flavors and smells. If you do not take care you could be able to lose them during drying.

To determine if your spices are dried you can contact them with your hands . If they break down without making your hands feel rough after this point, they are dried, but you should do not touch them.

breaking them up. It is better to dry whole leaves and seeds in whole pieces rather than fragments since they contain the majority of natural oils once they are intact.

They can be stored as they are without crushing them or dragging them whenever you wish to make use of them.

Dry herbs, whether spices or seasonings must be kept in airtight jars and containers. They must be kept away from direct sunlight as well as moisture and the heat. Do not keep them near the oven, or adding them to the food straight from the container when you cook. To help you to recognize various herbs, you should label the jars when packing them or after you have put the contents in them. The labels must contain the specific type of ingredient i.e. Dill. It is important to note the date you last preserved the ingredients so that you be aware of which herbs are old enough. This will let you decide which varieties you should first use. It is important to identify the various kinds of varieties using an eraser or by putting labelling on your jars, so you can utilize each for the proper use.

The flavors and spices that were not dried thoroughly are likely to dampen the containers, or turn rotten. In this case, you must examine the containers for a few days after pressing. If you observe any signs of moisture within the containers, you may dry them again and again put them in. All flavors and spices with molds must be discarded and shouldn't be used for any purpose. Important Tips:

Make sure to store dried herb in airtight pots and in plastic containers with zippers. Also, this is a good idea. Make use of small jars for canning, that will help keep the herbs in good shape for a long period of time.

Be sure to label every container with the date and name of the herb in the containers.

Transparent jars let you select the herbs quickly when you are familiar with them, however dark jars are more effective since they block the light.

The herbs will retain the majority of their flavor if you keep them in whole pieces, particularly the seeds and leaves. Keep them in their entirety and then crush them whenever you wish to make use of them.

Any herb that shows even the tiniest indications of molds must be thrown away. The herb containers should be kept in a cool, dry, and dry place far from dampness, heat and bright light.

The best dried herbs are when consumed within a year, unless they're whole, that may last for many years. That's when they're of maximum nutritional value. Dry herbs, that are older than one year, could have lost colour and flavor. Make a plan to dry and harvest herbs frequently and throw away old plants.

Freezing Herbs

The freezing of spices is another method to keep the spices. Spices that are full of dampness , such as many strong spices, such as Basil, Mint, Chives and Tarragon are best dried using dehydrators. Another alternative is to freeze the spices. It's easier to freeze them instead of dry them. You could consider freezing various spices such as Chervil Cilantro, Chervil Dill

List of Herbs: KITCHEN SPICES AND SEASONINGS

There are numerous flavors and flavors that you can utilize within your home kitchen. You can use the flavors and flavors in the way which you want and should not limit yourself to just what is mentioned when using these.

Dry Herbs and Spices

Have you ever mistaken coriander with cumin, or other flavors and spices? The next step is some of the spices you can find dry, store and dry.

Asafoetida: Asafoetida or Asafetida is usually used to aid with the assimilation process. It has a strong scent similar to the garlic-onion taste. It is commonly used for Indian cooking.

Achieve It is a bright, earthy-colored powder, or glue that is made from Annatto seeds (see under). It's a very hearty flavor. It is used to make Mexican food and condiments.

Allspice is a spice that has a similarity to Cloves and is a powerful and a sour taste. Used in zest mix.

Annatto Seeds Annatto Seeds are vibrant rosy earthy colored seeds that have a woodsy scent and a delicious taste. They are referred to as glue or Achieve powder (see the above) in the event of their grinding. They are used to enhance many Mexican food items.

Basil It is an individual belonging to the Mint family. Basil is green and has an incredibly sweet, Clove-like taste and a sharp. It is commonly used to make Italian and Mediterranean foods. The flavor is best with fish, chicken eggs, pasta, and tomatoes from a variety of types of food.

Straight Leaf: These are the sweet-smelling kind of leaves that come of the evergreen Bay shrub. They are often referred to as the shrub leaves. Straight Leaf is a woody, powerful taste. It is used in sauces, meats stews, soups, vegetables and can be used as a the base ingredient in many dishes.

Chili powder mix is composed of different herbs like dried chilies ground to powder, Coriander, Cumin, Garlic and Oregano as well as other spices and herbs. The flavor ranges from mild to spicy. It is used in Chili eggs, cheddar, eggs soups and stews.

Chives: Chives are rich and high in Vitamin An and have a place in the leek and onion families.

They possess garlic or onion flavor and are often used in tidbits and mixed greens sauces, shellfish, and cream soups, in addition to many other applications.

Cilantro is a green spices derived from Coriander plants. They are characterized by a strong scent that is lathery. They are used in smoothies and green juices as well as rice, fish as well as salsas and mixed greens. Cilantro is used to enhance flavor and seasoning. It is a well-known ingredient particularly in the preparation for Italian, Latin American and Mexican dishes.

Cinnamon Bark: This bark has been separated from Cinnamon tree. It has a dim, ruddy shading. Cinnamon sticks or ground are often added to foods items when cooking to give it flavor. It's sweet and incredibly deliciously fragrant. It is used to make desserts, doughnuts, and hot drinks. It is often added to vegetables like sweet potatoes, carrots as well as winter squash. Cinnamon can be found in a variety of different foods around the globe as sweet and tasty food items. Cloves have a sweet sweetness and a sharp and sweet taste. They are extremely delicious, and you must use them in a manner that is alert. They're earthy and rosy buds of the evergreen Clove tree. Cloves are used in baking in cakes to zest other treats for sauces, cooked beans, and also as pickling. They are great for braised meat.

Coriander The Coriander plant is associated to it being part of Parsley family. The seeds come out of Coriander. Coriander plant. Its flavor is a mix with Sage, Lemon, and Caraway flavor. It is a major used for Mexican and Spanish recipes, wieners, and in pickling.

Cumin Cumin: This is a hot, slightly unpleasant, and powerful. It is a common ingredient throughout Asian, Middle Eastern, and Mediterranean cuisines. It is commonly used in stews of beans and curry powders, as well as fish, sheep and picking.

Caraway Seeds The seeds are known for their anise-tasting flavors and are used in soft drink bread, potato dishes of sauerkrauts, and mixed greens. Cardamom is a sweet, warm spice that is used for the largest part of Indian cuisine. It is also used in baking, and often is mixed by Cloves or Cinnamon.

Cayenne Pepper: It's made from ground and dried Red Chili Peppers. It is often used in soups; zest mixes and braises, adding the flavor of hot, sweet. Chia Seeds While they're virtually flavorless but they can be crushed and added to oatmeal, smoothies, and other prepared foods to boost their nutritional value and to add the appearance of. They are frequently used as a replacement for eggs in vegetarian meals.

Coriander Seeds: They have an unnatural lemon-like taste. They are used in a variety of Mexican and Indian recipes for North African and Middle Eastern dishes.

Dill Seeds They are the seeds that come from Dill plants. They possess a tart and sharp taste, and are commonly used in meats, mixed vegetables sauces, and other vegetables. Dill Weed They are green leaves gathered in the form of Dill plants. They are tart and have a sharp flavor . They are commonly used in fish, eggs blended greens, sauces breads, pickling and vegetables.

Fennel Seeds The Fennel Seeds are earthy-green colored seeds that have been collected in Fennel plants. They have a delicate and fragrant sweet licorice flavors. They are often used in frankfurters, breads, soups, fish, sauces along with Italian dishes. They are chewed at once to refresh breath and improve digestion.

Fenugreek has a strong, consumed sugary taste and is used in a variety of Indian dishes as well as Middle Eastern dishes.

Garlic: It can be ground into a powder using garlic cloves that are dried out. It's used to impart the sweet, delicate garlic taste. Ginger: It is dried and then ground to produce a spicy flavor. Its Ginger root is slightly sweet, a little sharp, and has a strong scent. It is commonly used for German, Chinese, and Jamaican plans to prepare Ginger tea, sweets cakes, cakes, and marinades.

Lovage: This is an aroma that is similar to Celery or Parsley. It is used to flavor stock, fish as well as soups, mixed greens and soups in addition to pickling.

Marjoram is part of the Mint and Oregano family. The oval and light green leaves are aromatic, powerful and a bit harsh. They are used in dishes like chicken, meat, fish hotdogs, vegetables, as well as in fillings.

Mint: It's an extremely well-known zest that has an intense, sweet and refreshing flavor. It is used to rejuvenate beverages, and also in sheep, sauces soups, sweets, sauces and desserts. Mustard Seeds can be available in white, yellow and earthy tones. They possess a spicy sharp, sharp taste. They are used in cooking meats or pickling, as well as tastings. Finely powdered mustard can be used in sauces.

Nutmeg They are small seeds that have been collected from Nutmeg trees. They are a bit sour and have a slight shade. The Nutmeg seeds are warm and sweet and tangy. They are used for the preparation of drinks cakes, desserts sauces, and sweet potatoes.

Nutmeg is sweet and has an distinctive taste. It's a fantastic spice in cooked items as in savory dishes.

Oregano The Oregano is one of the members of Oregano: This is a member of the Mint family. It has a distinct scent, sweet and powerful marjoram-like or lemony taste since it's connected to the herb marjoram, as well as Thyme. Oregano is used in seafood, meat or poultry as well as tomatoes. It is a must when used in Greek, Italian, Mexican dishes, and Mediterranean recipes.

Paprika The Paprika is a red pepper that has been powdered. It has the sweet-hot and slightly bitter taste. It is often used in stews, sludges as well as fish, poultry and soups, as well as in egg and potato dishes that contain mixed vegetables. Twigs can be used as a garnish as well as in spice mixtures and in zesty blends.

Peppercorns: They're made from the peppercorn berries and can be found in a variety of colors. Dark, white and green hues are the most well-known. They are a striking spicy peppery flavor. They can be used to enhance poultry, eggs, and other meats.

Red Pepper: This is often referred to as Red Cayenne Pepper and its taste is spicy and hot. It is recommended to use it with caution, unless you enjoy extreme hot, spicy foods.

Rosemary: It is a silver-green leaves, and is part of the Mint family. Rosemary is a strong and piney taste. It is fantastic with barbecued fish, barbecued meats eggs as well as sheep, beans soups, stuffing and potatoes. The Saffron are the yellow-orange signs of disgrace (when dried) and are harvested from the crocus plants. It has a powerful sweet-smelling, sweet flavor. It is used in stews, sauces rice chicken, Spanish plans and Swedish cakes and breads. It provides food items with the radiant yellow color. Sage: It has small oval leaves, that have a slight greenish tint. It has a sour flavor and is used in chicken, pork wieners, ducks goose, and stuffing. Sage has a pine-like taste that is lemony and eucalyptus-like.

Sesame Seeds Sesame Seeds small, flat seeds that are red, brown or dark in shade. They have a slightly nutty and slightly sweet flavor and a smooth the surface. These seeds are often used in desserts, breads and cakes, salad dressings and seafood. Terragon has small sharp leaves that are dark in shade. The spice has a slight sweet licorice taste and is used in eggs, meats and poultry, pickling, mixed greens, sauces and other dishes.

Thyme The Thyme is an individual belonging to the Mint family, with small, green leaves. It The tea has a woodsy, smoky flavor. It can be used in fish, meats poultry, soups, and potatoes. Thyme is generally a useful seasoning. Turmeric: It is a yellow-orange root which is able to be crushed into powder once dry. It is a component of Ginger and used to enhance the flavor of food. It has a distinctive flavor, a bit woodsy, a little hearty and a bit sour taste. It is used in curries American mustard, and East Indian food. Turmeric is frequently used due to its yellow color rather than its flavor.

Some fresh herbs

You can use the spices in new dried or frozen flavorings and seasonings.

Basil: It has a sweet flavor that is used in pasta dishes or as a sandwich filling.

Chervil: It has an anise-like flavor that is numbing and is used in salads of mixed greens and for garnish.

Chives: They have an onion taste and are often used as garnish. Cilantro is a regrowth from coriander plants. The stems and leaves of the Cilantro plant taste powerful and are used to prepare Latin American, Caribbean, and Asian cuisines. Dill: It is a mild, fluffy spice that has a strong flavor. It can be used for picking as well as with fish as well as potatoes, among other things.

Fenugreek: It smells like maple syrup while it's cooked, but it is a different an intense flavor in the mouth, and can be consumed as sugar.

Marjoram: It's the scent of a woodsy flower and is often used in marinades and sauces.

Mint: It tastes very unusual and is often used in chocolate, chewing gum, and also with peas, sheep, and potatoes.

Oregano It is very lemony, and is commonly used as a flavoring in Mexican and Mediterranean recipes.

Parsley: It is a very well-known spice that is in the form of wavy or level. it has a delicate and rich flavor.

Rosemary: This is the flavor of pine and solid and is excellent in barbecued meat, eggs as well as beans and potatoes.

Sage has a piney flavor that is more like lemon and Eucalyptus.

Chapter 9: Advantages Of Herb Drying At Home

The herbs you dry at your home aren't only cheap, they are also more flavorful and powerful as compared to the dried herbs you purchase at the grocery store. Your food will be improved when you cook with the herbs you've dried. The herbs that you have dried at home are more fresh than the ones you can purchase at the local supermarket, which means they'll have more flavor. There will be less spice to create the taste you've always wanted from your grocery store spices.

Also, you will get the advantage of knowing precisely what is inside the package of spices. The majority of gardeners leave their herb gardens devoid of pesticides. Fertilizers are not usually required so your plants will be organic. It is possible to use compost that is natural to aid in the growth of your plants should you wish to. Manure from chickens is a fantastic natural fertilizer that can add nitrogen to the soil which will increase the production of leaf of plants. Pesticides aren't required to maintain herb gardens. The strong smell of plants act as natural repellent and keeps pests and bugs away. It's necessary to conduct some moderately controlled and you may have to get rid of slugs when the soil is overly moist in the spring time.

Because they are abundant and continue to grow after you've harvested a few of their leaves, you'll be able to have an abundance of herbs. It is possible to harvest the fresh plants from the garden to store the dried herb supply, or dry the pick. Many herbs are robust and can be planted in the springtime. They will begin for harvest within a couple of weeks and will continue produce all through the entire summer. Most plants will remain in good health until the first freeze. They self-seed, which means that, as plants become mature and grow, they shed seeds and new plants appear. It is rare to need to purchase new seeds after you've created your own herb gardens.

If you decide to plant dried and preserve your herbs you'll experience an elation and satisfaction. It's a wonderful sensation to head out to your garden and pick the fresh food that you can provide your family with. You can choose the most nutritious leaves, and to leave the ones that have wilted away. If you dry your herb plants, you are in full control on the quality of the herbs. There's no need to be concerned about other weeds or plants being thrown into the mix.

If you're not aware, spices and herbs contain numerous therapeutic properties and that's why so many people opt to cultivate their own in the first instance. If you or your family member is struggling to sleep Chamomile flowers steeped in water will aid you to relax. Lemon balm is a great option to treat wounds on the skin or used as a tea to alleviate the stomach upset. Parsley is a powerful herb that eases stomach constipation, as do peppermint leaves that are steeped in water. There are many things that you can plant in your garden of herbs that will enhance the taste of your food and make your body healthier.

Get your children engaged. It's a skill they will be able teach their children. Food preservation at home is a dying art which needs to be brought back! It is possible to teach our children how to save money which will be beneficial in the years to come.

The various ways of herb Drying

There are three methods for drying herbs however, drying herbs isn't restricted to the three methods. We'll discuss the most well-known three methods and then discuss a few of the other methods you can preserve the bounty of your garden. In general you'll want your plants to dry at temperatures of 100 degrees. Since most people do not have our homes that warm, you might need to look at other ways of drying your herbs.

Hanging/Air-Dry

This is among the most commonly used methods of drying herbs. It lets the herbs dry slowly and create the most wonderful aroma inside your home. The herbs are laid upside

down, either in a bag of paper or without ,
and allowed to dry over a period of 1 to 2
weeks based on the size of the batch which is
drying and the kind of plant. Some plants are
more moist than others. It's a risky
undertaking. If your house is too cold, the
plants will dry too quickly and you are at risk
of the growth of mould. We'll discuss ways
you can stop this from happening in the next
chapter.

Dehydrator

This is a fast and simple way to dry various
herbs in just a couple of hours. It is
recommended to select an dehydrator with
tray that is designed to hold tiny pieces of
herb that crumble and fall into the holes in
the tray. This method is popular however, you
could run the risk of losing some herbs due to
drying process being very quick. Some parts
of the plant will dry in a matter of hours,
while other parts will require longer. The ones

that dry fast will crumble to dust before drying process is finished. The initial cost of the dehydrator will be worth it when you frequently use it to dry vegetables, fruits and even meats. The dehydrator could be one of the most useful kitchen appliances.

Oven Drying

While it is possible to use an oven to dry your herbs it's extremely labor-intensive and can increase your electric cost. The majority of ovens don't have a setting that is low enough that allows you to put the herbs in a pan and then leave them inside the oven. Since the best way to dry herbs is at around 100°F and the average oven doesn't drop below 175, you'll have be watching the development of the herbs closely to make sure they don't dry too quickly or cause them to burn. Another option is to keep the door of your oven open for a couple of inches (yes it'll consume energy) however, it's almost the only method to maintain the temperature. A thermometer for the oven is useful and can give you an understanding of the internal temperature that the oven is at.

Solar Drying

Although this method can dry the herbs fast however, it will also eliminate the flavor of the leaves. This is not the most desirable method for drying herbs. The intense rays of the sun will cause the plants to bleach and cause the loss of taste, aroma, and therapeutic qualities of the plants. Drying your herbs in the sun on your porch or window facing south is an option when you're making use of the bunches for decoration reasons.

Microwave Drying

It is possible to use the microwave to dry herbs quickly to dry them if you're working in a rush. It's not the ideal method for herbs with a significant moisture content. It will require more effort from you and you could be taking about 15 minutes on the stove.

Drying of Refrigerators

Yes, it's difficult, however it could be achieved. The growth of mould will be slowed by storing the herbs in the refrigerator. It's a simple process and doesn't need any effort on your part other than place your herbs into the refrigerator for a few days and then take good care of them once they're dry. This is a fantastic alternative to parsley and chives as they go through a loss of taste during drying.

Each one of these options comes with pros and pros and. It is important to find the one that is suitable for you and your requirements. Explore a bit until you come across the one that is right for you. The next part, you'll be able to identify the different types of herbs and their moisture content which will allow you to decide the best method for each plant. Of course , there's an learning curve, however it's minimal and there's nothing you can do to cause harm to the plants you pick.

The Most Common and Easiest Herbs to Dry
tender herbs: They are plants with high moisture content and are more susceptible to mold. Basil, oreganoand chives, tarragonand chives are among the mint and lemon balm varieties.

Less tender herbs: They contain low moisture content and are able to be dried using hanging without worry about the possibility of mould. Thyme, rosemary, sage marjoram, summer savoury and parsley.

Herb flowers: Bee Balm Chamomile, chive Dill, geranium Lavender, linden marigold, nasturtium, Thyme and yarrow.

Herb leaves: bay celery Chervil, dill lemon balm, geranium lemon verbena, lovage rosemary, marjoram, oregano and sage. Summer sweet, tarragon, parsley and Thyme

Herb seeds: anise caraway and chervil. Celery, cumin, coriander and mustard

As you can see from some of the above lists Not all herbs are the leafy, green ones that you can find in the supermarket. There are a lot of "weeds" that actually are great flavor enhancers and are frequently utilized for their medicinal properties. Marigold, fever few , and even lavender are excellent plants that can be dried and stored.

Harvesting

Harvesting is an essential aspect of the drying process. You must pick the right season to ensure that you get the best flavor from your spice blends. For certain herbs, you can harvest portions of the leaves, while you let the tops of the plants remain in the process of maturing until seeds are set. The two herbs have seeds which are frequently utilized in kitchens. The cilantro seed is often referred to by its coriander name.

Other herbs, such as echinacea and chamomile, should hold off until your flower buds open and then pick. It is best to pick the flowers within a day or two after opening. This ensures that you have one of the strongest flower heads. The elements and the sun are slowly destroying flowers, diminishing the medicinal and aromatic qualities that the flowers possess.

For herbs with leaves It is recommended to collect the leaves shortly before the flower head begins to open. This will ensure that your leaves are bursting with all the flavor and aroma as you can. As the flower blooms and the plant is dedicating its energy to the flowering and seeding, and leaves will begin to fade.

Ideally, gardeners would like to harvest their plants early in the morning once drying of the dew. The majority of gardeners want to have the harvesting completed at 10 am in the morning. You'll want to capture the blossoms, leaves, and seeds before the sun has had a the chance to strike into the plants to take away its energy , and eventually, the flavor.

Don't harvest the plant unless you're prepared to begin the drying process immediately. It is not advisable to harvest and then let the plants in the kitchen countertop or inside the fridge for a few days. There will be a loss of flavor and put your plant at risk of mold. If you are able, only pick one type at each time. If you have only one day to complete the drying, be sure that you place the herbs in separate baskets so that you don't get them mixed.

If you're harvesting plants in the wild or even in your front yard, ensure that your plants haven't been exposed to pesticides, herbicides or animal urine or Faeces. Try to select plants that are located in an area that is enclosed.

How to Dry Herbs at Home, with minimal fuss, or the expense

Drying herbs is definitely one of the most efficient preservation techniques you'll encounter. It takes very little effort, time or even equipment. There is no need to monitor dry them or watch carefully the pressure or temperature like the case if you were making cans.

Before you start drying first, you must make your herb preparations. Remove any black or brown leaves. If the leaves are dying and yellowed, or look unkempt all around should be removed. Examine the plant for insect to see if there was someone brave enough to attack the fragrant herb. In the majority of cases it is not necessary to wash or rinse the plants. If you can you can, do not add any additional moisture to the plants. The plant could be swollen and increasing drying time. If you need to clean the plant, make use of cold water. Gently shake the plant to get rid of the most water possible.

Indoor Hanging

Hanging plants upside down inside can be accomplished in various methods.

Choice 1: This method is the best option for plants with high moisture. Utilize a rubber band or string to wrap around the stems of picked plants. It is advisable to make an bouquet of herbs. It is best to bundle one herb. If you are trying to save space by bundling many varieties of herbs can cause issues. Don't bundle more than 8-10 plants into a single bundle. A large number of plants can create a the inability to circulate air and increase the likelihood of mould growth. The drying process for all herbs is not at the same speed. For plants that are high in moisture you should make use of a paper bag in order to accelerate drying. It is important to let the process speedy so that you can avoid the growth of mould. You can cut a few holes into the bag in order to let air circulate.

The herbs should be placed with the flower's end pointed towards the bottom of the bag , and the stems inside the opening. Utilize a rubber band or string to secure the bag to the stems. Set the bag on a shelves of the pantry or in the area in the kitchen. Anywhere that the herbs are clear of direct sunlight and close to sources of humidity is ideal. The drying time of herbs can vary. Verify the condition of the herb after three days, and every day thereafter. The method of using a paper bag is perfect because it will capture the seeds and pieces of plant material that fall off during drying process.

Option 2. Follow the steps previously mentioned and do not utilize bags made of paper. The bag speed drying however it's not always needed for less tender herbs. Utilize a coat hanger or curtain rod for hanging the herbs. This method will give off an aroma that is pleasant as the herbs are dried. It's recommended to place the pan or plate underneath the bundles of dried herbs to catch any pieces that fall. If you're drying various kinds of herbs, you should put a separate dish under each bundle. The herbs are hard to tell when they are dried. The kitchen is the ideal location since it is one of the warmest rooms in the house.

Option 3: You could utilize an old, well-maintained window for drying your plants. If you don't have an older screenavailable, purchase screening material and spread it out across the rack. You'll need to turn the plants every day to ensure adequate air circulation. The screen can stop most of the dried pieces from getting through, but it's not bad to place a sheet of cookie sheets under the screen to collect any particles that get through. Make sure to leave ample space between the plants to allow for more air circulation. Keep the screen away from direct sunlight. The plants that you dry on the screen can curl. It's not a problem. If you're using screens, it's recommended to grind the dried herbs using this method.

Oven Drying

Set your oven to the lowest setting. If your oven is equipped with the warm feature, make use of the function to dry out your plants. Cover a cookie tray with parchment paper. Place the stems and leaves on the tray, making sure that there is enough space between each piece. Set the sheet on the bottom rack of the oven. Open the door to allow air circulation. The herbs should be checked at intervals of 15 and 20 minutes rotating frequently. Once the herbs are nearly to drying, switch off the oven, but keep the light on to let the herbs complete the drying process.

A different option would be to shut the oven on with only lighting on. This is ideal for sage, bay leaves and mint plant. Put them on towel. Add another towel to the top. Add the leaves in a second layer. This can be done with up to five layers. Carefully place the paper towel along with the leaves on the oven rack and then close the door. Let it sit overnight. The next day the leaves should have dried sufficiently to store.

You could also make use of an old screen from a window on your woodstove in the winter months to dry your herb plants. Your home will be scented with the scent of your drying herbs. The screen needs to be placed on cast iron cups or pots to prevent the herbs from being placed directly in the oven.

Dehydrator

A dehydrator is and easy method of drying lots of herbs at once. If you purchased the dehydrator brand new, it's likely to include a manual that outlines the different options and drying times for your plants. Certain dehydrators are more expensive than others, and they will differ in the control options available. If your dehydrator has an adjustable temperature setting, you can choose at between 95 and 115 degrees. If you live in an area that has high humidity then you should raise the temperature to the temperature of 125 degrees. Put the herbs on the tray. It is recommended to have the same variety of herbs on each tray to ensure that they don't get mixed. Based on the type of dehydrator you have the process can vary between one and four hours.

Refrigerator

Allow the herbs to completely dry by letting them dry at the table for about an hour. If they are wet, the herbs in the refrigerator can mold! The herbs should be placed on a cookie sheet. You should ensure that there is enough space between each one. Place the dish in the refrigerator while it is open, and allow it to sit for around an entire week. Herbs that have been dried in the fridge tend to retain their color better than dried using other methods. You can also place the herbs in a plastic bag and let them dry. This can last anywhere from one to two weeks.

Solar Drying

The sun is definitely an effective method of drying your herbs, however it's just a little hot to be soft. If you plan to use the sun's rays for drying your plants you'll need to tie them around the stems similar to how that you would use for indoor drying. Hang your herbs upside down on your balcony or any other railing that receives direct sunlight. It's helpful by wrapping the herb in cheesecloth in order to stop animals from munching on your food. Also, you can utilize the paper bags from the drying room indoors. This will usually take approximately three days.

Microwave

This technique is not recommended for plants with a high levels of moisture, such as mint. To dry the leaves in the microwave, take the leaves from their stems and lay them on a towel. Put a towel over the leaves, then place them in the microwave. Nuke on high for one minute. Allow the herbs to rest for 30 seconds prior to taking another 30 seconds of nuking. Switch the duration between 30 secs on and off for 30 seconds until the herbs are dry. This could take as long as 10 minutes.

Herbs Once You Dry Them

Your work isn't done after you've harvested your dried herbs! Now comes the storage of your herbs. You could want to organize your herbs in several ways. The herbs are dried enough to be suitable for storage when they fall apart when you rub them between fingers. Do not crush them all at once while you test dryness.

Ground

This is the standard type you can find within your home kitchen. We purchase ground spices from the market and then mix them into our meals. The process of grinding herbs is simple. You can place the stems and leaves into the Ziploc bag and then use the rolling pin to smash the leaves. Another option is using a morter and pestle. They are relatively inexpensive and are readily available at the local pharmacy. You can grind a few leaves and stems at a time , making sure that you've got everything ground. The time to store ground spices can range between 6 months and 2 years.

Whole Leaves

Leaves are more flavorful when they aren't crushed to store them. If possible, keep the leaves as whole and grind only before making use of. This will ensure you get plenty of flavor. Whole leaves can be stored for up to five years. Leafy herbs can be stored for 3 to 2 years.

Seeds

Seeds are best stored in their original state. If you require ground seed to prepare a recipe or tea but do not crush until just before you use. Seeds are good to store for between 2 and five years. They are usually utilized in their entirety. You can also use dried seeds to grow new herbs to grow in the garden.

Flowers

When drying the flowers will begin to wilt and fade in colour. Avoid crushing the flowers until prepared to utilize them. They will become fragile. Try to take care of them until you are prepared to use the flowers.

Storage Methods

Jars-You can use mason jars that are sealed by a lid and band. This is a cost-effective option to store dried herbs without having to buy many fancy containers. Dry thoroughly and sterilize the jars prior to adding the dried spices.

* BagsZiploc bags are an alternative. You can spend the money on high-quality bags. If the bags fail to close completely, the air will cause

your herbs to deteriorate. Bags are a great choice for small amounts.

* Plastic containers - Plastic bowls and containers with an airtight lid are an alternative. However, it is best to choose small container or bowls. Closing and opening the container to take a handful of herbs can result in the herb losing their potency due to the constant contact with air.

* Old spice jars/containers-Those spice jars you have sitting in your cupboard can be cleaned out and reused. They're ideal for your needs , with proper lids that make it easy to shake them out enough.

After you've placed your herbs in a container or bag, mark immediately. It's too easy to lose track of which herb went where, and you may end in mixing the herbs. Label the container to ensure you are able to follow the proper rotation.

If you're a fan of a particular blend, such as Italian seasoning or an Mexican seasoning mix, make several blends and store them in containers. This will allow you to save time when making your favorite recipes. You've probably tried spiceing your food and are aware of what your family and you would like to eat.

Don't store dried herbs over the stove, or in a cupboard near the dishwasher or stove. The heat and humidity can reduce shelf's lifespan. A cool, dark , and dry area is your ideal choice. Check your dried herbs regularly to ensure that they don't have moisture. Condensation in the sealed jar indicates that the herbs were not dry. If you notice that there is mold growing it is time to remove the plants. If there isn't any mould then you can repeat the drying process over again and save your plants.

It is vital to note the fact that dried herb is between three and four times more powerful as fresh ones. If you're following a recipe which requires fresh herbs, and you are using dried herbs be aware of this.

For teas, you can use one teaspoon to a tablespoon of the herb to make a cup. Sprinkle hot water on the ground herb and let them sit for up to 10 minutes. You could use ground herbs as well as whole leaves. You can check the effectiveness of dried herbs by sniffing them. If you still can smell the scent from the plants, then the dried herbs are safe to utilize. Even if it is impossible to detect the scent of the herb, it will not get rotten. It is still a viable option however it might have small aroma or flavor.

Chapter 10: Herb Gardening: The Essentials

We hear and see numerous references to the word "herbal" But have you taken the time to consider what "herbal" is, and what exactly an herb is? For starters the word "herbal" simply means "Made by plants" It doesn't matter if it's soap, food, or drugs. However, this doesn't mean that it's made of herbs. What exactly are they? The term 'herbs is a reference to flowers which grow above the ground and do not usually turn into woody. They are prized for their flavor, medicinal properties, and fragrance, in addition to other benefits. Cambridge dictionary describes an herb as species of plant that has leaves utilized for the preparation of medicines and cooking, to add flavors to various meals.

Herbs are most likely the most well-known and fascinating collection of plants that has been around throughout time because of the different ways in which they've been utilized. For instance, they've been used to flavor food scenting our bodies and homes as well as for decorating gardens and houses as well as curing illnesses they impact all aspects the way we conduct our daily lives. Are you contemplating cultivating your own herbs for one of the reasons I just mentioned? I'm sure the answer is yes , or you wouldn't be here.

It is possible to grow organic herbs in your backyard with very simple steps that we will discuss throughout this publication. The additional benefit of organically growing your herbs is that it helps you stay clear of harmful chemicals that are that are found in herbicides and pesticides that are common in traditional gardening.

Herbs are grown in a different manner from other plants in regards to the techniques used for the cultivation process, the conditions that are required as well as the kind of plant you intend to cultivate. Let's have a look at the kinds of herbs you can cultivate in your garden prior to discuss how to establish a successful herb garden.

Herbs of various types

There are many kinds of plants inside your yard. Here are some of herbs:

Culinary herbs

These are the herbs you can incorporate into your meals to give it a flavor. These include thyme, sage mint, parsley, parsley and basil.

Aromatic herbs

They are used for their smell , but not for their taste. It is possible to make a variety of herbs in order to create diverse concoctions for fragrances, air fresheners sprays as well as deodorants (which are also able to be made for your dog). There are many such as rosemary marjoram, lovage, and rosemary and lovage, just to name few of the most popular.

Ornamental herbs

This kind of herb is chosen to enhance their appearance and beauty. They can improve the look of your garden more appealing. They are mainly chicory and valerian.

Annual and perennial herbs

The perennial herbs are chives spearmint, southernwood and French thyme. They are cultivated in the form of spreads. This means you must plant them at least a few inches than each other in order to allow them the space they need to develop.

However, the annual herbs like marjoram, basil, coriander and savory exhibit the tendency to increase in size and spread, making it beneficial to have small spaces. They are relatively simple to cultivate in a typical soil types.

It is important to note that many herbs are developed from seeds. This is why you must be aware of the kind of herb you would like to cultivate prior to making any other decisions.

Benefits and Uses of Herbs What You Can Benefit From Herbs: Why You Should Maintain Your Garden Your Own Herb Garden Herbs have been utilized in numerous ways, like flavoring food as well as perfuming our homes and bodies, adorning our homes and gardens, as well as helping to treat certain diseases, which affects the entirety that we live. Let's explore the benefits more deeply.

The herb and its seeds can be utilized in numerous different areas, from therapeutic to spiritual and culinary applications. For instance, you could make use of herbs to soothe insects, allergies, arthritis, diabetes, asthma and blood pressure, hypertension and to reduce cancer symptoms.

If you're planning to have your own plant that you can plant outside it will surely add a beautiful touch to your backyard or your garden. Many herbs look as gorgeous as flowers and shrubs and you can include them to your garden in the event that you don't have space for an elaborate herb garden as they blend beautifully.

Incorporating herbs into your diet will increase the vitamin content of your diet plan , which makes the herbs extremely healthy.

Planting your own garden will save you money. It is the first step to save the expense of going to the store and the time to search for the kind of herb you'd like to buy.

Planting your own herbs will give you tips on the art of gardening as well as new and improved recipes.

Some herbs have extremely strong aromas which are calming and rejuvenating. They also help to relax the muscles of the brain. Some herbs are also used in the detoxification, therapeutic purposes in addition to weight loss.

In most cases the local market may have a small selection of plants, meaning you're only able to purchase the items that are offered. In contrast If you have your private garden, you can grow any herbs you like.

If you're convinced you need to create the herb gardens of your dreams, we can discuss how to plant the herbs you'd like to cultivate inside your yard. Let's begin by talking about the requirements you'll need to grow your herb garden.

The conditions required for growing herbs

When you are planning to grow any plant, you should first understand the conditions that it needs to flourish. The same is true for growing herbs.

Herbs that favor shades such as mint and sweet woodruff also prefer a woodland-like, moist environment.

*Mediterranean herbs such as oregano and lavender are suited to slightly less fertile soil in full sun and in warm temperatures.

*Annual herbaceous plants, such as basil, dill, chervil and coriander, prefer full sun however they require a bit more water or else they will simply stop seeding.

The conditions needed to grow differ from plant to plant. All other plants have 3 common conditions for growth with the only a few plants that prefer shade. These conditions comprise:

Sunshine Sunlight and slightly lean soil is believed to trigger the production of oils and the scent and taste of the herbs to increase. Herbs that are grown in rich soil or surrounded by an abundance of food can become smaller and less fragrant and flavor. However, plants that are used for flowering must be provided with plenty of soil that is rich and water.

Regular water and good drainage Regular Water and Good Drainage: Many plants do not like to have their roots wet or constantly moist soil. This means you have to make sure that there isn't a lot of water in the soil, which could lead in root rot and cause the plant to weaken and consequently invite diseases.

To determine the way your soil drains water, create the hole roughly as big as a gallon-sized jug in your garden. Fill it with water, allowing the water to run out. After the water has been completely removed then fill the hole with water and take note of the time it takes to be drained. If you find that the water can take more than eight hours for it to go down, it's essential to find an improvement in the drainage

Regular trimming and harvesting to keep them full Most gardeners don't have the time to cut their plants. It is possible that if you are growing your herbs for use cutting and trimming won't be an issue. If you don't cut and make use of your herbs, they'll get too big and lean, and the annual plants will begin to sprout much more quickly. Even perennial plants with woody leaves like rosemary, lavender and sage will get bigger and will have smaller dead wood when they are cut every year at least.

Now that you are aware of the requirements required to grow your herbs, we can begin to prepare your garden.

Garden Preparation

Before planting the herb you want to plant You must ensure that you have the right preparations and an understanding of the methods you can employ to do this. Here is a method to help you organize your garden:

1. Set up your garden

For beginners it is recommended to grow the most basic, commonly utilized herbs like basil parsley, sage oregano, chive and thyme. Also, you should consult with experts to determine what the conditions in which where you intend to plant the herb is suitable.

Once you have obtained the desired seeds or seedlings of the herb you want to plant then prepare the soil for planting. Herbs thrive in a range of soil kinds. Making sure your garden is prepared makes it much more efficient, resulting in greater results from your herb.

The the preparation process for your garden can include the testing of its fertility and texture. This will guarantee that you are in a position to take the necessary actions to make your soil suitable for growing your plant. The application of organic fertilizers may not immediately show results, but, over time, you'll start to see an improvement in both quality and quantity.

2. Techniques for soil preparation

To have a beautiful garden, you must have a good soil. The way you prepare it can help ensure that it is perfect. To ensure the growth of herbs, good soil must comprise fifty percent of solids as well as 50 percent of porous areas that allow vital growth elements like water, air as well as the root systems of plants to penetrate. The solid portion of 50% is composed of organic matter as well as tiny rocks. You can make use of materials such as ground corncobs and hay, sawdust, straw, bark chips as well as cover crop which can add nutrition to soil. It is possible to use spades to mix the ingredients with the soil.

PH

It is also possible to test your soil for nutrient levels and identify any insufficient nutrients that are essential for development of plants. In the event of needing to boost the nitrogen content it is possible to increase the amount of the fertilizers suggested. The pH (acid alkaline) of your soil should be likewise assessed (on an scale from 1-14, one is the most acidic, while 14 is the one with the highest neutral and alkaline, while 7 is the most acidic) Most herbs flourish when the pH is between 6.5 to 7.5. The PH number determines if the majority of the vital nutrients found in the soil are accessible. The pH can be adjusted in your soil increasing or decreasing the amount of ammonium in the soil by using sulfur products. In this situation you could add agricultural lime if the pH is below the pH recommended and if the pH rises over 7.3 it is recommended to utilize sulfur to lower the pH.

Fertilizing

When it comes to fertilizers, you could select to use organic and organic fertilisers. Organic fertilizers are recommended to be healthier and resistant plants. Some organic fertilizers also contain the same nutrients as soil, but they have a different structure. They function in a similar like manner to the soil's natural nutrients. Organic fertilizers, on other hand, are made from the waste of animals and plants. They typically take time to become effective because microorganisms first have to take them apart. Manure is a good option because it is a bulky material to improve the soil's texture and increase intake of nutrition in the soil. The addition of inorganic fertilizer is a good idea for instant absorption of nutrients.

For a successful fertilization of your garden, employ the use of fertilizers that are broadcast. This basically means you'll need spread the fertilizer over your entire garden , based on the suggestions of the particular herb you have chosen for the purpose of spreading the particles evenly, mix the fertilizer in the soil, and then smooth your soil in the process to prepare for planting. It is also possible to enrich the soil following planting by feeding your herbs with a dressing (digging trenches around plants) and then applying fertilizer to make it easier for plants to take it in.

Composting

Recycling is also a means to improve soil quality to plant and grow plants. This is accomplished by reusing the kitchen and garden waste. This helps speed the process naturally of decay by dissolving organic material and the components that are then returned to soil. The presence of moisture, proximity and the air circulation of the pile accelerate the process. The transformed organic wastes and plants such as humus can provide nutrients to the developing plants and enhance the soil's capacity to regulate water. This could reduce the amount you have used on soil conditioners, fertilizers and also time since you have a place to get rid of lawn, weeds, and other garden waste.

If the compost is dark brown hue, it is able to be used in potting soil to aid in gardening seeds to protect seeds from the scorching drying sun. Compost can also be useful in reducing soil moisture, or increasing the capacity of water to hold in sandy soils as well as in clay soil. In fact, it is the ideal to improve drainage. You can also make use of leftovers from your kitchen as fruit peels, vegetables tealeaves, coffee grounds, tea grounds and eggshells.

Microorganisms

It is important to remember that soil microorganisms are able to break down compost i.e. they simply break down complex substances into simpler substances that the plants are able to utilize however they do not create nutrients. Microorganisms living in soil are at their most active when temperatures exceed 60 degrees Fahrenheit. the majority of them performing best in a moist and alkaline atmosphere. Microorganisms usually work rapidly on organic matter that is small. There are two types of microorganisms: those which require oxygen in order to function (aerobic) and those that don't require oxygen (anaerobic). There is a way to produce compost inside an airtight container because of microorganisms that do not require air. This is why covering a trashcan with a tight seal during winter is a great way to convert your kitchen organic food waste into compost in the winter. The compost pile outside needs to be re-circulated frequently (about every two weeks) using a pitchfork in order to supply air for the microorganisms that require it. The various composting tools that are on the market have distinct advantages, however it is important to keep in mind that you don't really need any fancy equipment to create compost. A basic container made from old cinder blocks or fencing material is ideal. The bin could be either square, rectangular or round and placed in a corner, but close enough to the gardens. It should be between four and five feet wide and three feet tall.

These are the basic steps to follow for composting that can be successful:

Start with a 1 to two-foot pile of leaves , or 6-12 inches, or greater of material that is compact such as sawdust or grass clippings straw, compost hay, nuts, hulls, or trimmings from trees (except the walnut). They will generally take longer to break down unless they're cut up. You can also make use of any type of kitchen garbage (except the meat waste) and make sure they are free of chemicals or pests.

The top layer of this pile the next layer must be a fertilizer. Nitrogen will help in activating microorganisms that will accelerate the decomposition of organic matter. Add around half a cup of limestone from earth (most microorganisms love their environment sweet). You can then add a couple of shovelfuls of garden soil. This will create a starting point of microorganisms. It's beneficial to keep a small amount of soil nearby as you start your compost pile.

The heap should be well-watered. The heap must be kept damp, similar to an untried sponge. Continue to accumulate garden waste until the top of the pile, as the space becomes accessible. When the layers are thickened and compacted, duplicate the layers of lime, fertilizer and soil.

Every two weeks, about once rotate and mix the stack using an axe or digging fork. This will ensure that all of the elements that make up the compost pile, not only the core, get heated. As the temperature of the compost pile rises, harmful bacteria are killed and the process of decay cannot be slowed.

Strategies For Growing

Indoor and outdoor gardens

After you've decided on the plants you'd like to cultivate take into consideration whether you'll plant them indoors or out in the open. There are a variety of methods for growing herbs depending on whether you are indoors or outside. Indoor herb gardens offer a all year-round growth and there are no herbicides. But, they yield less yields than the outdoor ones. Outdoor gardens are only in use for a some seasons and require weeding, but they will yield more because the space isn't so limited as the indoor garden (although this will depend on where your garden is located).

The amount of sunlight required will depend depending on what species. For example, chives as well as sage love sunlight, therefore planting them in a location that receives enough sun is crucial. Try to make use of natural light as when you use it instead of artificial lighting you reduce your energy use and also reduce the environmental impact.

For planting outdoors herb gardens, they are grown in a formal arrangement. They can be cultivated in rows with other crops in your garden. There are however some exceptions, such as mint, which may grow if not controlled. Therefore, they prefer to be grown in containers or in separate areas where their spread can be restricted.

When you plant, make sure that you plant tall plants at the edges of your garden, with plants with medium height in the middle and shorter ones towards the front to provide your herbs the greatest exposure to sunlight. It is best to do this by writing down the lighting, soil and water requirements, and any other unusual growth patterns that you observe.

Techniques for Planting and Growing

When and how to plant herbs

Herbs don't require specific any specific timeframe or season for growth since the conditions they require can be adapted to suit the time of year or season. In addition, they do not require a lot of attention so long as enough sunlight, water, and the balance of pH are maintained. Selecting the right herbs to plant in a suitable environment that is humid, moist, sun-drenched or dry can allow for the growth of the plant, general aeration among plants, and spread.

If you're beginning your herb garden from seeds make sure to purchase the seed starter potting soil that is not enhanced by adding additional nutrients as seeds block the nutrients they require to germinate and grow. To plant seedlings, make sure you select potting soil with no pesticides applied for treatment. But, you can compost using commercial soil to aid in helping the plants to grow strong and healthy.

Start early in spring. The best time to plant seeds is when the temperatures are at a minimum, are cool as well as the season is yet to begin. The seeds are given the chance to germinate and be fit to be planted.

Seed preparation must be placed in containers that are labeled (any kind of container that is small, such as an egg carton from the past or containers you can buy at the local nursery or yogurt containers). Label the containers so that you be aware of the seed you're planting. Fill the containers with potting soil, then dampen the soil by adding a small amount of water and place them in a bright place with a constant temperature about 70 degrees. In the early stages the seeds shouldn't receive long periods of direct sunlight or they could overheat.

If you do plan to plant your herbs outside it's easier to plant seeds indoors because you are able to control the temperature as well as the water. Also, you should know that many herbs require a moist and humid environment to sprout. So, if your area of residence is dry you should make use of a plastic wrap protect the pots of seeds. Be sure to not cover them too tightly as the seeds need air circulation to grow. When you are in a position to plant the seed soak the seeds in good condition to sprout. Place the seeds on two moist paper towels in an even layer , and allow them to soak for approximately 4 hours before the day you plan to plant them.

Start the seed, but make sure that you look over the seed packages to find out how each type of plant is to be planted. Some seeds require a scattering on the soil's surface, others will not sprout in the absence of covering them. In the coming weeks they will start to grow and begin to grow and produce leaves. Make sure that the sun and temperature are in check, and ensure that the soil never has the chance of drying out. If the seedlings begin to develop leaves, it is necessary to take a few seedlings from the ports in order to let the more robust ones expand. Remove the seedlings with less development and leave around 1 inch room between remaining plants. This is known as thinning the seedlings. With an agro rake, loosen up the dirt and then rake it into the soil mix you purchased for your herbs up to about 6 inches. In small quantities, add water to keep it moist, and make holes about inches apart to get ready for planting the plants. But, if you're intending to plant this in pots, you need to know the amount of herbs you will fit into each pot. Many herbs can be quite big when they grow, so placing more than two plants in each pot can cause congestion over time.

Weeding Pruning And Watering

To maximize the benefits from the growing and planting procedure, you must consider small areas to pay attention to, which comprise:

Regularly Prunning

Pruning is the removal of weak and infested foliage and stems often to create an herb that is more bushy towards the future. The result will be blooming, which signals the beginning of an upcoming season.

Weeding

This is the act of eliminating unwanted plants in your herb garden to ward off weak roots and insects. This is also done to increase the healthy growth and leaves. Regularly watering your herbs however, on a timetable so that your plants can dry out between watering sessions are crucial to ensuring healthy conditions for growth. If you are using chemical treatments to eliminate pests and diseases watering your garden regularly could play a significant contribution to decreasing amounts of residual that could be left at the top of plants when harvesting.

Protection of herbs from pests and diseases

Insects and diseases that are present in herbs may cause you to not get the desired results regarding healthy and beneficial herbs. However many herbs have essential and aromatic oils that act as natural repellents to various kinds of insects, which can destroy the majority species of plants.

Pests

However, pests such as snails and slugs may get access to your garden and ruin your plants. These are the major slugs that cause trouble. Although they rarely cause any major harm, they can cause problem and must be addressed to prevent damaging the appearance of your yard due to the slime trails, especially when you are planning to plant some herbs for the beautification of your yard or lawn.

Aphids are fond of tender and young leaves. They usually induce curling in the leaves and cause sooty mould which in turn draws the ants. They usually reside in dense, fast-growing herbaceous plants. To prevent this plant from becoming overcrowded, spacing your plants could assist in a major way. You could also make use of neem oil and other garden soaps to combat the aphids.

If spider mites attack (these are typical when it is hot and dry) make sure you use a large flow of water in order to flush the mites out.

The leafhoppers can also attack your parsley, basil and oregano, so keep an eye out for them if growing these plants.

Other pests that can affect your garden are whiteflies, parsley worms the leafminers and flea beetles weevilsand spittlebugs.

Health Conditions

The majority of diseases in herbs are caused by soils that are waterlogged. They can trigger fungal diseases such as furasium root decay which manifests as brown streaks on stems of the herb that lead to the plant falling. However, certain herbs like lemongrass and mint are not affected by large amounts of water, and therefore are at less risk of developing fungal illnesses.

The mint family is largely affected by rust. It manifests as brown, rusty lesions on the leaves' underside.

The most effective way to safeguard your herb garden from disease and pests is by creating appropriate conditions for growing pruning, sanitation, and pruning (such as the raised bed method that encourages drainage that is good) and watering during the morning hours to reduce growth of fungalspores that aid in spreading diseases.

In addition it is essential to ensure that you pick healthy plants to plant, so that you can plant them with plenty of space, and follow the correct irrigation and fertilization. Also, make sure that you do not get bored of trimming (harvesting) as it is an excellent natural method to make sure you take away any unhealthy foliage and remove any pests that could be residing in your garden. Also, you will notice that your plants tend to keep producing (becomes more lush and bushier) as you cut them back especially after you have removed the blooms. You don't wish to see them blooming because this is usually the end of the season.

Take note that if you're already using chemical treatments to treat your skin, stop immediately since most herbs are cleaned and used fresh. Another issue to the use of chemicals is that the herbs may be harmful or harmful to the consumer. If it's necessary to use chemicals to treat an untreated issue, ensure that the label of the chemical is suitable for eating.

Harvesting Herbs

There are many reasons to picking herbs at different seasons. But, they are typically harvested when the oils that give the flavor and aroma are at their highest. But, it is all dependent on the purpose of use and the specific plant part that you will be harvesting.

The best time to harvest is in the morning, after the dew has gone away and before the sun's scorching heat of the day.

If it's intended for the foliage, it is best to harvest it prior to the blooming that is, prior to the time when flowering starts as it could cause a bad flavor or a decrease in leaf production. Also, it has plenty of foliage and you can harvest around 75% of this year's growth in one go. In essence, herbs possess the best flavor right before blooming This is why this is the ideal time to harvest.

When harvesting herbs in order to preserve the herbs for future use ensure that the plant has reached its most aromatic. Harvest it early in the morning, when the aroma is at its best during the day.

For health reasons If you can clean the plant every day prior to harvesting.

It is important to be conscious that when you harvest seeds that the harvesting time needs to be exact enough to allow the seeds to fully ripen but they should be picked prior to their dispersal i.e. when harvesting seeds you must wait for the seeds to turn from dark brown to gray before they break open. The herbs you can harvest this way include borage and chamomile. The best method to ensure that seeds don't spread without your knowledge prior to harvesting is to watch on a regular basis. After that, harvest when the seeds are removed. Cut off the heads and place them in a large paper bag. Allow them to drop straight into the appropriate place that you've set up. Then, keep your bag for your drying. Make sure you don't compress the seeds heads. It is essential to ensure you provide sufficient air around the seed heads so that you can reduce or completely eliminate the possibility of mold forming.

What do you do if you are unable to maintain that watchful eye? Do you depend on luck to harvest plants after months of growth? You don't need to. You can put the seeds in a bag head (while still in the plant) in a small mesh bag or paper) after the flowering has finished and the green seeds are visible. After the heads have dried then any seeds that fall out will be stored inside the bag. When you see that seeds are released and falling out, cut the head, bag and everything else and then dry them in the in the indoors.

Take note of whether plants are biennials, perennials or annuals. Also note how big you can expect each one to be when it reaches maturity. Be aware that certain herbs, such as chilies can be attractive in bloom.

It is best to collect herbs like chicory, bloodroot, goldenseal and ginseng as the leaves begin to fade. If you are harvesting them for crafts, then you should pick them just before they've fully opened.

Conserving Herbs

Herbs acquire their flavor and aroma from oils. They do this by smashing them, meaning that it evaporates into the atmosphere, and then loses the flavor and aroma with the passing of time. This is why knowing how to keep them safe is essential if you wish to utilize these herbs for over a period of weeks, days or even months after harvesting , without worrying about loss of the flavors and oils.

Hang drying

The most commonly used method of preservation of herbs is through hang drying.

Freezing

Freezing is among the most effective methods to preserve herbs. It's quick and simple and also the flavor is generally more freshly picked than when dried. If you have space in your freezer, then freezing is probably the best method to cook herbs. It is best to do this by washing the herbs, shaking off any excess water, and then chop them up finely before placing them on the ice cubes filled with water prior to freezing. After that you can place them in bags of paper and seal them. However, when they are thawed, they can't be used as garnishes, however, they can be used for cooking as they won't appear like they did when you harvested them. Also, you should not freeze the herbs once they have thawed.

Drying

Drying is a traditional method of preservation that you can apply to your plants. Its benefit is that it is done without effort and all over the world without fear of ruining the herbs. If the plants are clean then you can clean them off using a cloth but don't soak them in water and then shake off the excess water and then place them on a towel to dry the water on the surface. After this then you can take out any damaged or dead foliage and then tie the stems into small , loose bundles that allow for the air to circulate around each group. Then, hang them upside down in a dry, warm and well-ventilated area, far from sun as the sun's rays can damage as UV rays together with dew create a haze and reduces the potency of the herbs. Some of the places you can dry your herbs include huge cupboards, kitchen pantry, and even barn. Some of the herbs that can dry this way include sage and spring savory and dill and parsley. Basil and mints, as well as tarragon could discolor and mold when not dried in a timely manner. Another method of drying is to spread the entire bunch over window screens. Just hang the screens on your chairs' backs, and rotate them frequently to ensure they're drying.

For seeds, place them on a piece of paper with holes punched into the sides. Then, hang them in a dark area that has good circulation of air. Once they have dried and are stored in rigid containers that are lightproof to prevent contamination.

It is also possible to opt for the microwave drying method, which is an easy and quick method of drying a small amount of plants. Place a single layer of dry, clean leaves between dry paper towels and then put on the stove for one to 2 minutes at high. Drying time will differ based on the amount of moisture in the plant and the wattage of the microwave. The leaves should cool. If they're not too stiff, microwave them for 30 seconds, then retest. Repeat as required. Keep in mind that herbs with long leaves may require to air dry for a few days prior to microwaving.

Herbs are dry enough when they're brittle and break easily. When the leaves are dry then you can remove them from their stems, put them into containers that have lids that fit tightly. The best containers are either hard glass or plastic. You can, however, utilize zip-lock bags made of heavy-duty plastic. To keep their taste don't grind the leaf until you are ready to make use of the leaves. Keep dry herbs in cool, dry location far from sunlight and heat.

A variety of herbs can be stored for up to a year if they are kept in a proper manner. However, you must be aware that certain herbs are prone to lose their flavor after exposure to air , however they may retain their aroma and flavor when stored in alcohol or oil. While certain herbs will retain their flavor if stored correctly, some herbs do not retain their flavor regardless of how they are preserved. Hence for those who want to retain the flavor of the herb it is essential to make use of fresh. But, that doesn't mean they're impossible to use them for longer, because you can extend their seasons by growing them in indoor pot plants during winter season.

Chapter 11: Techniques For Drying

There are a variety of ways dried herbs can be dry. Certain methods employ modern equipment like the oven or food dehydrator, while other methods are more traditional and were employed by our forefathers. We'll discuss more in the future about the signs that your herbs are dry, and what method you should choose to suit your particular situation and dried herbs. Let's go over each method separately.

Before beginning the process of drying, ensure that you shake any insects or dirt off the herb. You can clean your herbs if you have to, afterward, pat dry. This is a fantastic tip to spray your plants using the watering hose in the evening prior to harvesting, you don't need to clean the plants as thoroughly before drying.

If you don't have to clean the plants, it's not recommended to wash them because any moisture added to them will hinder drying. Get rid of any sickly or wilting looking leaves prior to drying your herbs. You may choose to cut off the stems, or leave them in. A lot of people prefer to add the stems since they are often more flavorful than the leaves, however this is completely dependent on your own personal preferences.

Air Drying

Drying herbs in the air is the oldest method for keeping herbs. It typically involves hanging the herbs on a hanger or lying on the ground to dry. Herbs with a natural low in moisture are ideal options for drying by air. Sage and oregano are two examples of commonly used herbs with low moisture which you can air dry. There are a few benefits to using this method. It does not require gas or electricity which makes it very affordable. Another advantage is that dry air provides a low-heat method to dry plants, which aids in keep the levels high of essential oils.

Materials required for air drying

Fresh herbs

The kitchen string (rubber bands can also be used)

Paper bags

Hanging hook or any other item that you are able to hang things from

The rack for cooling cookies or the herb drying screen

Cotton towels or paper towels

It is possible to require needles and thread

How do I Dry the Air? Dry

If your plants have stems that are long and can easily be arranged in the shape of small bouquets and are suitable to hang. Just attach a string to the small bouquet. Keep in mind that the bigger the bundle you create the longer it'll be drying. It is advisable to bundle together not more than ten stems.

The plants are now in good condition to hang however, many prefer to make the extra effort of placing a bag made of paper around the plants. The result may not appear like a beautiful arrangement however it shields the plants from sun and dust and also catches any seeds or leaves which fall. For the method of a paper bag begin by poking or tearing holes into the bag, so that air circulates around the plants. Then, slowly place your bundle in the bag and leave the stems loosely away. Then, tie the bag to the stems, then hang.

Label the bag on the spot or hang a label on the bag if you're concerned about losing track of which herb belongs to which. Be aware that some of them appear different when they're dry! The date should be written down. It's an effective method, and will help you remember to get them off when they're done. Make sure you hang your herbs in a place which is dry and warm such as a basement, garage or porch is unlikely to perform due to more humidity. The same goes for laundry rooms or bathrooms. A dry attic (no roofing leaks!) can often be very useful. It is recommended to have a dark space but you can use it to have some sunlight. If your herbs are close to a window that is sunny be sure to keep them from overheating by drawing curtains or blinds and also using the method of the paper bag.

The bundles can be hung on a hook or nail, or a string that is strung between two points or, sometimes, using a push pin. It is also possible to be creative and create a chandelier the mantle of an unloved fireplaceor the hanging racks of closets or the lower parts of your kitchen overhead cabinets or any other location that you like. In the event that you own a bed with a canopy you could use it! While you search for drying spaces make sure you keep in mind that air circulation and low humidity are crucial.

For leaves that are large and have stems no stems utilize the needle and thread for stringing the leaves separately. Set aside two or 3 inches space between the leaves. you can hang them until they dry.

If you're drying plants which aren't ideal to hang, like small plants or leaves you could utilize a cookie rack in order to dry the herbs. Since cookie cooling racks are not designed to handle small herbs, it is best be sure to protect the rack by covering it with newspaper or cotton towel , and then place the herbs on top. Dishcloths made of flour are ideal for this. When drying flower petals big enough to be supported by the wires in the rack for cooling, slide the stem into the rack and let the flower to rest on the wires on top as the stem hangs. Be sure to label your racks to ensure that you can identify which plants are which when they're dried.

There are also drying racks that can be found at the web and in some department stores. These are typically a wood or plastic structure that is hung or placed on the counter with a smaller gauge screens to put your herbs over. They can be folded down and easily store when they are not being used. If you are a fan of DIY projects, search online for directions on how to build your own drying racks for your herbs - there are many innovative solutions available made of upcycled materials, such as broken windows and photo frames.

In the event that you do not have access racks, it's acceptable to lay your herbs flat on a towel paper towel and place them in the drying room. This will take longer as there is no air circulation underneath but it's a good option in the event that there is no moisture in the air.

As you will see, air drying is easy. It takes around a week for the majority of herbs to dry using this way. In the case of drying something more substantial like the seed pod It could take a few weeks to dry completely.

Sun Drying

In the majority of cases sun drying may not be the ideal method. The scorching sun could cause the burning out oil essential to your plant and also, the light can bleach the color of your plants. In the end, you'll have dried leaves that are dull and without odor. Sun drying can be very difficult when you're working outdoors because of the changing temperatures and levels of humidity.

For certain items you might want dried, sun drying may be the most effective option. If it is done correctly it's a simple method of drying herbs as well as a dry method that is low-cost because it does not require gas or electricity.

Materials Required for Sun Drying

Fresh herbs

A colander or other ventilated container

The rack for cooling cookies or the herb drying screen

A second screen or cheesecloth

Cotton towels or paper towels

How to Dry Your Sun

There are many different ways to dry your plants in the sun. The first one is easy making use of a colander, or container that lets air flow. Colanders work well for the majority of herbs. If the herbs are tiny and are slipping across the gaps, just line the colander with cheesecloth or paper towel. Other containers that could be suitable include shallow terra cotta planter dishes that have drainage holes.

The herbs should be placed inside the pot in one layer, and place the container in direct sunlight of the window. If you intend to let the herbs out to dry, make sure to cover the container by cheesecloth or another screen. The container must be well covered in order to stop birds and insects from taking your herb plants. Drying your herbs outdoors is only recommended If you have several consecutive sunny and warm and dry days that have low moisture in the region. Bring the drying container inside during the night.

Another option is to use racks instead of the container. This is like air drying. It is possible to lay the herbs on a paper or cookie drying rack, and cover them with cotton or paper towel. Make sure they're in one layer. After that, you can put them over with another screening or cheesecloth. If using cheesecloth make sure you attach it to the rack so that birds or winds aren't able to be able to pull it away. The rack will still require bringing the rack into the room the evening. Racks can also be carried out indoors using windows that let in lots of light throughout the daytime. Many people hang an adjustable drying rack inside the window to accomplish this.

Also, if drying multiple herbs at the same time, make sure to label them to help you identify what herbs belong to which once drying. When drying in sun, it can take anywhere from a few days to one week for the majority of herbs.

Food Dehydrator Drying

Utilizing an appliance for food drying is among the most effective ways to dry herbs. It is for one, the temperature level is simple to regulate by turning an adjustment dial to reach the temperature you want. It's not the same for the sun and air drying. Additionally those layers are the most of space. Additionally, you can put the dehydrator in virtually every space in the house even though high humidity could be a factor in drying times. Another benefit of drying with a dehydrator is that you don't need to fret as much about putting too much moisture on your herbs after washing them . simply shake off the excess moisture you can while the dryer will get rid of the tiny droplets that remain. The most significant benefit is that it can be done in a matter of hours rather than days.

The downside of using the food dehydrator is that it comes with higher costs as compared to sun drying or air. It is possible to find a dehydrator at under $50. If you're looking to splash out there are elegant dehydrators that are priced at more than hundred dollars. However, you do not need to have all of the bells and bells. Of course, there will be electric costs when operating an appliance particularly if you're making several batches. Dehydrators are surprisingly efficient and you won't be able to tell the difference on the cost of electricity.

Materials Required for Drying in Dehydrators

Fresh herbs

Food dehydrators with vented racks

The Dehydrator Drying Method

Drying herb in the dryer is easy, however, there might be some uncertainty with the temperature setting. The drying process should begin by setting the temperature to 95 degrees (Fahrenheit) in the area of low humidity. If the humidity is higher, begin at 115 °. Examine the herbs every 30 minutes. If you do not notice noticeable shifts in the herb within two hours, this could be an indication that drying is taking more time than it should. You might need to increase the temperature. You could reach 130 degrees. Based on the type of herbs that you're drying, the whole process can take from one hour to four hours. Check the manual for your dehydrator for more information.

Preparing your herbs involves arranging them in an even layer on drying racks. If you're drying a variety of kinds of herbs at same time, don't combine them on one rack. Some will take longer in comparison to others and you'll need to be able remove the rack after one type of herb is dried. If you are drying a variety of herbs, it's a good idea to write down the order in which you put the racks. For instance, you could write"Top rack - oregano, middle rack – bay leaves Bottom rack - basil. You might be amazed at the different appearance of your herbs in only two hours!

Oven Drying

Conclusion

Herbs were used throughout the ages in various cultures to provide the medicinal value as well as nutritional. With the development of modern medicine and became more common, herbs became less popular. Many people are still looking to return to fundamentals. They don't want to be taking chemical supplements all day long or experience the negative consequences of prescription medication.

Prescription and over-the counter medication can be costly for customers. For those who require regular medication, it could be a major burden for their finances. Being able to feel better in a cost-effective manner is essential.

If you can cultivate and dry your own herbs, they are significantly less expensive than the products you buy. If you plant perennial varieties of herbs, you'll only need to pay one time to start. They will then grow again and again every year, for you. If you harvest them properly and maintain them by supplying them with sun and water they will thrive.

You also have total control of their quality. Don't assume that the herb you purchase, or the ones available at the farmer's market are grown in the most favorable conditions.

The research shows that the bulk of the dried herb products for purchase aren't certified organic. They were cultivated using pesticides that are contaminated with harmful chemicals. Organically certified plants organic are more expensive.

If you purchase dried herb in bottles they've been exposed to radiation in the majority of cases. That means they've been exposed to some form of radiation called gamma. It's done to eliminate any trace of pathogens. But, this procedure could also decrease the effectiveness of the herb.

The data that we can access today suggests that by taking treatment of your body at an earlier stage in life, you'll be able to lower the risk of developing health issues later in life. Who would like until 100 and be in such a state of health that they cannot have a good time? It is best to be able to enjoy the golden years and be as healthy as is possible.

Drying your own herbs could give you the tools to combat and prevent different health issues. Prevention is an important element of the health puzzle that is often neglected. Most people don't think about the body until they fall sick or have grave issues such as heart disease or cancer.

It is our duty to care for our bodies. Do not blame your genes and give it up to chance. Utilizing these herbs is the most effective and simple method of improving your health today and prevent serious health issues later on.

Find a couple of plants that can help with your specific requirements. Spend the time to find out about their benefits and how best to make use of these herbs. Learn how to cultivate your plants using the most efficient and efficient methods. In addition discover the best methods to gather them effectively.

Examine a variety of drying methods to pick one that is suitable for your specific needs. Be aware that certain varieties of herbs perform better using one method of drying in comparison to others. Your personal preferences play a an important role in the way you choose to do.

Check that the herbs are dried for use later. Place them in airtight glass containers or glass jars with labels. You can then reach for the herbs whenever you require the herbs without any issues or problems.

You will create many possibilities for you and your family members by growing the herbs you want to dry. Preventative care can reduce your risk of developing illness and enable you to live living life to the maximum!